JOINING IN

AN ANTHOLOGY OF AUDIENCE PARTICIPATION STORIES & HOW TO TELL THEM

COMPILED BY TERESA MILLER
WITH ASSISTANCE FROM ANNE PELLOWSKI

EDITED BY NORMA LIVO

INTRODUCTION BY LAURA SIMMS

YELLOW MOON PRESS
CAMBRIDGE, MASSACHUSETTS

ISBN: 0-938756-21-4

Music Notation & Calligraphy by Susan Kano
Artwork for "The Princess and the Ogre" & "Paper Flower" by Will McDonald.
Cover Photo © Tom Raymond,
Production Editor - Lyda Kuth
Production Assistance by Anna Warrock
Production & Design by Robert B. Smyth

We are grateful to the following for permission to reprint previously published material.
"The Freedom Bird" © David Holt. High Windy Productions.
"Bracelets" adapted from *School Before Six - A Manual for Nursery School Teachers*, © 1971 Laurel Hodgden.
"Paper Flower" © 1988 Fran Stallings.
"In Summer I Die" © 1985 Doug Lipman.
"Rabbit At The Waterhole" © 1988 Linda Goss.
"Juan Bobo and Sisi" © 1981 Gail Neary Herman.
"The Magic Wings: A TALE FROM CHINA," by Diane Wolkstein. Text © 1983 by Diane Wolkstein. Reprinted by permission of the publisher E.P. Dutton, a division of New American Library.
"The Little Blue Alarm," adapted from "Six Thousand Alarm Clocks" from *Curious Tales* by Milos Macourek.
"The Princess and the Ogre," adapted from "A Puzzling Story" by Natalie Babbitt.
"Some Thoughts on Audience Participation" © 1988 Heather Forest.

Publication of this book has been made possible in part by a grant from the Massachusetts Council on the Arts and Humanities.

Yellow Moon Press
P.O. Box 1316
Cambridge, MA 02238
(617) 776 -2230

CONTENTS

Preface - Teresa Miller

Introduction - Laura Simms

Carol Birch
BRACELETS   1

Heather Forest
THE LION AND THE RABBIT   5

Linda Goss
RABBIT AT THE WATERHOLE   9

Bill Harley
THE FREEDOM BIRD   19

Gail Herman
JUAN BOBO AND SISI   23

Ruthilde Kronberg
WILLIWU,
THE LONELY LITTLE WITCHGIRL   31

Kaye Lindauer
THE PRINCESS
AND THE OGRE   39

Doug Lipman
RIDDLE STORY:
IN SUMMER, I DIE   49

Norma Livo
HOW RACCOONS
GOT THEIR MASKS   55

Teresa Miller
THE LITTLE BLUE
ALARM CLOCK   59

Anne Pellowski
MRS. MONDRY
AND HER LITTLE DOG   67

John Porcino
THAT WAS GOOD!
OR WAS IT?!   71

Barbara Reed
HOW ANANSI
GOT THE STORIES   75

George Shannon
LAZY PETER   89

Laura Simms
SUNMAN   95

Fran Stallings
PAPER FLOWER   99

Ruth Stotter
AGA-BOOG-A-WAY
X-NAY-SNAZE-NAY   105

Diane Wolkstein
THE MAGIC WINGS   111

NOTES ON THE CONTRIBUTORS   119

PREFACE

One morning I woke up with a thought; I shook my husband awake to share it. "You know, "I said. "I've just been a lot of flotsam on the ocean of life. It took storytelling to finally give me direction."

And it is true. Storytelling revived interests I had considered long gone. However, the child within never disappears completely; it is always waiting to burst out with the joy of being alive on this earth. It took *stories* to transform me into a wave that flows peacefully for the most part—sometimes splashing high, sometimes crashing down—but pulled by a deeper current rather than bumping along on top of the ocean, never belonging here or there.

In the process of becoming one who tells as well as listens to stories, I attended many workshops, watched many storytellers, read many books, and listened to albums and cassettes. I still do. For I am only beginning to understand what draws me to the activity of storytelling, and to uncover all that it has to offer.

Among my most wonderful moments in this world of storytelling are those of "participation," in which the teller engages the audience directly in the telling. For me, no joy equals that of having a group of individuals, with their imaginations as their sole means of transportation, enter a totally new world, all together.

When I first discovered this delight, I searched in vain for a book that addressed itself primarily to this aspect of storytelling. Although I found several compilations that included participation stories, such as those by Virginia Tashjian and Bernice Wells Carlson, not one book on this subject appeared to be in print. *Joining In* had to happen. Happily, several of America's leading storytellers shared my interest in making it happen as well.

Like any journey through life, the process of getting this book into print has been a series of starts and stops, with changes of direction, and yet always the support and encouragement of a few to keep the spark alive.

In this book the tellers share not only the stories, but their experience telling them. The guidelines they provide are the result of having told the stories many times over and incorporating what works best for involving the audience in the telling. Eventually, being the creative individual you are, you will work out your own methods of enticing the audience to join in. Trust your instincts. Make the changes you sense will improve your telling. Go with the pros in the beginning, though; it will give you more confidence later with your own personal alterations and adaptations.

For me, the next best thing to sending this book off to do its job will be to see it in actual use. So, if you're ever in my area telling one of the stories, drop me a line. You can count on me to be there—JOINING IN !

Teresa Miller
August, 1988

INTRODUCTION

It is with great pleasure that I write an introduction to a book of participation stories. I have had the pleasure of co-creating tales with audiences young and old for the past twenty years. Repeatedly in situations that might be impossible (distractions, discipline problems, unsuitable environment for storytelling), it has always been the telling of a "joining in" story that would break the ice and bring the audience together in a dynamic and fruitful listening.

Terry Miller has persistently and cheerfully compiled these stories and notes from many different storytellers in much the same way she put together an abundant public garden in Queens. It is my hope that my thoughts will add water to further their growth. We owe her great thanks. It is with much thought, however, that I write this introduction; for the performance of "joining in" stories, which is so spontaneous and capable of profound benefit, is unfamiliar and challenging, particularly to a new storyteller.

The tradition of participation stories is ageless and known to most cultures. A storytelling occasion can include spoken, sung or incanted words, dance, songs, sound effects, poetry, call and response, theatre and musical accompaniment. Such events are considered vital to the health of individuals, the community and the environment. Some of the benefits of this style of performance include: bringing people together, engendering happiness, instilling social responsibility, heightening awareness, synchronizing mind and body, and renewing one's sense of the sacred in the everyday world.

Participation stories are irresistible. Many years ago I attended a concert performed by Ephat Mujuru, a traditional storyteller-singer from Zimbabwe. He performed his native African stories in English and in the Shona language to a sold-out audience of adults in New York City. He told a story about a man who was attacked by wild animals while walking in a forest. The man began to run. When he was surrounded he stopped. He remembered his mbira (a thumb piano) and he began to play music. As he played music and sang his song, the animals became enchanted. One by one they began to dance. Unseen by the animals, the man escaped.

As Ephat told the story he sang a refrain for the man. It was soft and fearful. Beckoned gently we began to sing it with him. The storyteller smiled to encourage us. He did not need to instruct us to sing the song at different times in the story. As each animal appeared Ephat made a sound for it. Spontaneously we repeated the sound of each animal. We became the animal and we became the animal becoming enchanted. When the man remembered his mbira we sang his refrain louder, becoming more confident and joyous. We were the man, we were the animals; we helped the storyteller, we enjoyed ourselves. In essence, we tamed the wild beast in each of us while unabashedly dancing the animal spirit in our hearts.

That evening, with each new story, we improved our ability as audience. Because we took part so wholeheartedly, we heard the nuances of rhythm and meaning and intention of the performance more clearly. This more precise participation encouraged Ephat to speak more effortlessly, and with more poetry. At one point he was so pleased with our response that he stood up and danced. No verbal thanks could have expressed his gratitude for the strength and inspiration we gave to him and to his stories. It was obvious to everyone that the relationship between teller and audience in storytelling is powerful, mutual, and deeply essential.

We could have gone on and on for hours tirelessly. The energy stimulated in this reciprocal activity was like a wellspring. We had tapped into something ancient and limitless. Next he told a long and complex story. Our ears were finely tuned. The call and response story had reminded us how to listen viscerally to any tale whether it included outward response or not. When a storyteller invites the listeners to reverberate the sounds of the story, the audience's combined answer is stronger than any individual's answer. Harnessed to the story by the presence of the teller, we could whinny and neigh and ride freely in response. At the same time, we had the delightful satisfaction of consciously supporting the creation of the event.

In truth, any storytelling is a mutual creation between the teller and their audience. This is the uniqueness of oral narrative. The real story is the one that arises from the active imaginations of everyone involved. However, these stories demand a different skill from the performer. They require great energy and humor and improvisation. It is well worth the extra effort. I will try to give some how-to hints and examples based on my own experience to help elucidate what is needed from the narrator.

My first experience with the power of call and response story was in a junior high school in Roosevelt, Long Island, New York. During a two-hour lunch break the students pushed back tables and chairs and made the cafeteria into a dance space. The boys straddled the chairs, using the wooden seats for drums. As they played pulsing, intricate rhythms the girls formed circles and began to move in patterns, adding syncopated hand-clapping. Here were the echoes of their grandparents' games from the south, and here was the memory of a powerful African tradition. The room was filled with individual pride, a sense of fun, and communal respect. In this school they had few discipline problems.

I learned a great deal from that experience. I began to incorporate songs, gestures, and hand-clapping in my stories with the young students. My acceptance and utilization of their input made them eager to hear more stories and to write their own. Also, I learned that although my audience was more than willing to take part, it was up to me to make the right invitation and up to me to keep the integrity of the story forthcoming. If I had memorized the story with the gestures, and repeated it by rote rather than by heart, I would lose my connection with them. Their response would be half-hearted because they knew I was more involved with *my* story than with the one we were making together. My telling always had to be fresh. In other words, I had to know my story well, but be open to accept their responses as well as orchestrate them so the whole situation worked.

The awareness and vitality that is called for on the part of the teller is a particularly challenging task for a beginner. You might ask, how can you learn a story by heart and not by rote? First of all, in live performance the words are only one part of the story—the content or the plot. The meaning and intention, the breath and response of the teller is another, while the imaginative and psychological response of the audience is the third.

Here are some suggestions on how to learn and practice an audience participation story: Make a map of the events to see where the "joining in" takes place. And make an outline of the sequence of events so you can walk through your story and not merely the words of the text. The basic structure of the story will inform your performance in other ways as well. Knowing when and where you are to call the audience into the story will help you keep the narrative in harness and give you the cues to vary a rhythm or modulate an effect that reflects the meaning or mood of the unfolding tale. Often the map will reveal the significance of the participation. It will let you know if it is included for fun, to emphasize a point, to mime a characteristic or emotion, or to increase the intensity of the events. If you insist on memorizing, do all these things first so that you are invested in the words. In this way you can get hold of the reins of the story and then begin to concentrate on the audience.

The energy has a lot of momentum. If you know the events, and the meaning and landscape of the story clearly (not necessarily the words of the text), it will be your protection from becoming confused. One suggestion is that when starting out, you might learn the story and tell it without the gestures or the songs a few times to become certain of what takes place in the story, and what your style and rhythm are.

Try the sound and gestures out loud before you tell the story. If you are not comfortable with the suggestions given here by professional tellers, make your own, but first try out their ideas. The clearer you are the more confidently the audience will respond. If your audiences are shy at first, don't worry. Let them see that you enjoy the story. In their minds they will take part. The next time they will venture out. The storyteller's enjoyment, or willingness to be foolish or to make a mistake, becomes the best encouragement for others to dive into the unfolding tale, courageously and unabashedly.

Recently, in an inner-city afterschool center a child sat in front of me, expressionless. His sadness was a wall separating him from all the other children and myself. He did not join in. However, he watched me like a hawk. I began to put more energy into my story, trusting that he was wanting to get involved. Finally, his arms went up and his face became animated. It was obvious that he had forgotten his self-consciousness. Soon he was smiling and moving. The teachers and administrators present all watched in astonishment. Catching their eyes, I urged them to lift their arms and join in.

Taking part in these stories not only inspires confidence, it is actual practice in taking part in our lives and in the world. Part of the satisfaction is the unspoken realization on the part of the audience that they are supporting the story, actually making it happen. Part of the delight is the compassion generated from the interdependence of everyone present.

Just as that evening many years ago in New York between Ephat and his audience, or just between myself and myriads of audiences of all ages throughout the world, including children's schools, theater festivals, adult concerts, and the most inconceivable situations—a decaying ballroom in a homeless hotel, or an outside event in the Bronx Zoo—it is the audience who gives power and substance to the story. In their response, whether out loud or silently from the unspoken cornucopia of the imagination, is the amplification of the event with more energy and life than a single person can provide. You have merely to look at the faces before you to see that we are taking part in genuine creation.

An ancient text in India says that "the universe hangs on sound." A Hopi myth warns that what enlivens the heart of the earth and of man is a song sung by twins reverberating through the axis of the world. A Bushman myth relates how a boy saves his village through his song. Raven, the Innuit god of creation, experienced sorrow at the death of a friend. He danced alone on a beach. Not until he began to sing did he acknowledge his despair and begin to feel joy. Then he flew away.

A "joining in" story is like a sacred incantation. The repetition and building intensity take the audience out of themselves. The uplifted feeling of being carried by the story refreshes mind and heart. For a Navaho Singer, the beauty of the music is in its usefulness, its capacity to benefit. It is assumed that when the chanting is wholehearted it can restore harmony within an individual, between people and their environment, and control supernatural forces. I think this is true for a participatory story well told.

The experience of participation truly generates happiness. When we concentrate on the story and become responsible for bringing it alive, it takes us out of the concerns we have in our everyday life. There is renewed creative energy to find alternative ideas and meaning in one's life. The sound of the stories reconnects us to the song inherent in everything. And perhaps one benefit, which we usually associate with the content of the story rather than the act of telling it, is that joining in generates social responsibility by reminding us we are able to respond. I hope you will enjoy these stories and take the challenge of telling them from your heart.

Laura Simms
August, 1988

ADAPTED BY
CAROL L. BIRCH

Bracelets

NARRATIVE	AUDIENCE RESPONSE OR TELLER'S ACTION

Ellin's birthday was coming, and her mother asked her, "What do you want for your birthday?"

"I'd like a bracelet," she said.

"Okay," said her mother, "What else do you want?"

"Can I have another bracelet?"

"Yes, of course," said her mom, "but is that all you want this year—just bracelets?"

Nod your head affirmatively, and smile broadly.

So her birthday arrived. Ellin opened the first package. Inside was a beautiful bracelet. She put it on. She opened the second package; inside was a silver bracelet. She put it on. She opened a third package, and inside was a gold bracelet, so she put it on, also.

Speaking directly, ask the audience: "What do you say when someone gives you a present?" They will chime in with, "Thank you!"

Ellin looked at her mother and said, "More."

Speaking in a low, willful and slightly malevolent tone.

And Ellin's mother, being a good Fairfield County mother [insert the name of any community that is known for over-indulgence and/or the community in which you are telling this], went out and bought her more bracelets. She bought spangling, jangling bracelets that came all the way up and up her arm.

Move your hands up and up your own arm.

Her mother went out and bought her plastic bracelets. You know, you've seen them—purple, orange, green, blue, yellow, red, fuchsia, and polka-dotted bracelets that came all the way up and up and up her arm.

Moving out into the audience, move your hand up and up a child's arm.

"MORE."

Ellin's mother put bracelets up and up and up and up both legs!

In the audience, move your hands from the ankles to just above the knees of a child.

1

"MORE!"

Ellin's mother put bracelets up over her body, up over her neck, up over her mouth!

"That's enough."

But Ellin's mother couldn't hear her, so she put the bracelets up and up and up.

Ellin stood there, covered with bracelets. And, she sneezed. "AHHHH CHOOO!"

When she sneezed, she lost her balance. When she lost her balance, she fell down and broke every single bracelet.

Ellin got up, and dusted herself off, and went to see her mother.

"MOTHER!" she said. "Next year for my birthday, I'd like to have a necklace—JUST ONE, PLEASE!"

Usually, a child who is sitting with legs extended is a good choice.

Although I normally put my hands around a child's waist, after that I stop using a member of the audience, stand quite straight wherever I am am in the midst of the audience, and move my hands in a mime of stacking bracelets over my own chest, neck and mouth.

You'll need to whisper this in one of those loud but hushed whispers that carry, because children will be yelling out, "MORE." After they notice your stillness, and how your body is holding the tension of the moment, they will get quiet and you can repeat—while peering over your hands that are just above your mouth—"That's enough!"

Mime the stacking of bracelets up your face and over the top of your head.

To make much of in mime and to enjoy.

NOTES

Here is a story that is an excellent example of how stories get passed on "orally." I heard it from Diane Wolkstein, who heard it from one of her students, who got it from the author Laurel Hodgden, a psychologist with the Headstart Program in Ithaca, N.Y. who wrote it as part of a Headstart grant in 1971.

"Bracelets," like most stories, is more than the sum of its words. It is particularly effective for beginning and closing programs, because of its brevity and its levity. It is exhilarating as it reveals, and revels in, unabashed greed. It surprises audiences by jarring their expectations for traditional, once-upon-a-time conventions: It is modern in tone. It occurs in present time. It is set in their community with the insert ". . . being a good [Fairfield County, or L.A., or Madison] mother." It is rife with consumerism. This is not a fairy tale! Like the tales of Dr. Seuss and other modern, comedic fables, the situation becomes inflated, extreme, and, therefore, it invites a "fall." One of the joys for me, though, is that Ellin is "brought down" but remains undaunted. Audience participation in this tale is responsive. It does not require the kind of instruction that often backfires in the telling and leaves participants feeling more isolated and self-conscious than ever. In "Bracelets" it is virtually impossible to keep children from saying "MORE!"—more energetically with each occasion. Pause, savor, build the excitement by leading yourself and your audience up to the breaking point of comedic tension.

"Bracelets" is a story to have fun with! Because I use "Bracelets" primarily as an ice breaker, or piece to close with after longer, more demanding tales, I do not build a program of "like" stories around it. It is possible to continue with stories of greed, self-centeredness, overabundance, or humorous disasters. But I am opposed, generally, to the usual narrow approach in "theme" programs. They tend to be stifling in a singularity of vision that borders on didacticism. Similar stories are often alike in rhythm and tone and that becomes a real obstacle in performance and in the structure of a program. Susan Cooper, the writer, suggested that fictive worlds entertain by offering refreshment, solace, excitement, relaxation and, perhaps, inspiration[*]. I would suggest that an effective storytelling program provides much the same variety of experience. Programs rich in contrasts of rhythm, tone, style, intention, and subtext are my preference. Learning a story because it "fits into the theme of the program" is a sorry reason to choose a story. How much better to say: This one will be refreshing after that last one, or, after that frightening tale, this story will be a comfort.

---

[*] Cooper, Susan. "Escaping Into Ourselves," in *Celebrating Children's Books*.

The Lion and the Rabbit ...a Fable from India

Introduction

In my introduction to this tale, I invite the audience to portray the "echo" in the story. We rehearse the concept of an audience being an echo by my singing or saying odd sounds and phrases, and, upon my gesturing to "come along," the audience "echoes" them back. I point out that the echo is one of the most important parts of the story and encourage the audience to listen carefully for when "echo" enters the tale.

NARRATIVE	AUDIENCE RESPONSE OR TELLER'S ACTION
In a jungle in India, long ago, there lived a ferocious lion. He roamed the jungle and killed for pleasure! He killed more animals than he needed to eat. The animals lived in terror of the beast, so they went to the lion with a plan.	
"Oh, Lion, King of the Jungle," they cried, "if you will stop your unnecessary killing, the animals have all agreed to send you one animal each day to be your supper. Think of it! You will never need to hunt again, for one animal each day shall come willingly to your den."	
"Agreed!" roared the lion, "but that creature must come at the proper time. I do not like to wait for my dinner!"	
The animals sent a wise old rabbit to be the lion's meal. As the rabbit went along the road to the lion's den, he walked very slowly. By the time he arrived at the lion's den it was late, and the lion was hungry.	
"Why are you late!" he roared. "You've made me wait!"	
"Your Majesty," said the rabbit, "I'm late but it was not my fault. I was detained by a wicked ferocious lion. I can picture him now. He had long, sharp, claws . . . like yours . . . a swishing tail . . . like yours . . . frightening teeth and a huge mane . . . like yours!"	
The lion went into a rage. "Another lion in MY jungle! Take me to him!!!"	

"Then come with me," said the rabbit, "and I will show you the most wicked, most ferocious lion in this jungle."

The clever rabbit led the lion to a deep well that was filled with water. He pointed down into the well and said, "Look in here your Majesty, and you will see the most wicked lion in the jungle."

The lion stalked the well, looked down into it, and saw his own reflection in the water. Thinking it was another lion, he roared a terrible roar.

"R-O-A-RRRR!" The sound of his roar resounded in the well and bounced back at him as an echo.

Having rehearsed the audience's part of being the "echo" in this tale, gesture to audience to join in with an echo: "R-O-A-R!"

"Who are you?" he roared, and echo answered . . .

"Who are you?"

"I am the King of this jungle!" And echo answered . . .

"I am the King of this Jungle!"

"No you're not, I am the King!"

"No you're not, I am the King!"

"One more word and I'll attack!"

"One more word and I'll attack!"

"R-O-A-RRRRR!"

"R-O-A-RRRRR!"

And with that the lion became so enraged, with claws spread wide, and sharp teeth showing, he charged into the well with a great splash!

The wise old rabbit went back to the other animals to tell them that the wicked lion had attacked his own reflection . . . and would never be heard from again.

NOTES

Cultures everywhere have stories which are "fables," tales in which animals talk and act out the foibles of human beings. Often these tales are straightforward and have a clear moral. This type of teaching tale can inspire discussion and insight into the issues raised in the story.

"The Lion and The Rabbit" is one of many ancient fables attributed to a storyteller named Bidpai who wrote them in Sanskrit over 1,700 years ago. *The Tales of Bidpai* have been translated into languages around the world through the centuries. Other collections of fables from India are *Panchatantra* and *The Jataka Tales*. Many of Aesop's fables can be traced back to themes in these ancient sources.

A contemporary adaptation of a section of the tales of Bidpai, as retold by Ramsay Wood, is *Kalila and Dimna: Selected Fables of Bidpai* (New York: Alfred A. Knopf, 1980).

Some Thoughts on Audience Participation

Listening to a story is not a passive experience. It is an action-filled, colorful event in the theatre of the mind. Storytelling, by its nature, is an audience-involving artform. As the storyteller's narrative, shared in words and gestures, is perceived by the listener, vivid images are created in the listener's imagination. Costumes, scenery, characters, come to life with as much complexity and detail as the creative listener devises. Even when the teller shares stories with a large group, there is an intimacy and an immediacy to the artform that bonds the teller and the listener as the journey of the tale unfolds. The teller holds the attention of the listener with the suspense of the tale, painting, prodding, and cajoling the visualization. This can be an active and delight-filled experience for the listener who can vicariously imagine to be all things and all characters in the tale. Since the imaging on the part of the listener is rooted in their own personal imagination, the transfer of the tale is both a group event and a highly intimate exchange between the teller and each listener. There are as many stories being heard as there are ears to hear the teller.

There are other formats for audience participation in a storytelling event beyond a solo teller involving the listener's imagination. The possibilities are diverse. Suggestions from the audience could help to shape an improvised tale. Members of the audience could join the teller in the performance space to assist with the telling, a prop, or to act out the tale as it is told. Or, the whole audience could join in the telling at times, giving voice or motion to a repeatable refrain, a sound effect, a song or a rhythm. The possibilities are unlimited.

I prefer to suggest that the teller experiment with sound and motion in rehearsal and performance until motifs that are effective are found. Trial and error can be fine teachers. Images in stories can conjure any number of abstract sounds or motions on the part of the teller. Likewise, sounds and motions can conjure images. Assuming that the storyteller is a creative person who is willing to explore a wide range of possibilities in sound and motion, there are unlimited voice and body images that can be rooted in the teller's imagination and then shared in the telling.

ADAPTED BY
LINDA GOSS

Rabbit at the Waterhole

NARRATIVE

AUDIENCE RESPONSE OR TELLER'S ACTION

STORY! STORYTELLING TIME! STORY! STORY-
TELLING TIME! AYE YEYE YEYEYEAH! AYE YEYE
YEYEYEAH!

I need you to help me tell a story. We are going to travel
to Kenya. Kenya is a country in East Africa and it is the
place where Sungura the Rabbit lives. I (the storyteller)
have here my goody-bag and inside my goody-bag, all
kinds of magical cloths that I use to help tell my stories.
But I am going to need about five volunteers to come up
here and help me. Who wants to help out? Raise your
hands.

The storyteller chooses
five volunteers to be
the Sun, Wind, Water,
Grasses, and Night.

This cloth will be the Sun. The next cloth will represent
the Wind (SHSHshshshiuuuu!) The next one represents
the Water. (It's raining, it's pouring, the old man is
snoring. Rain, rain, go away. Come again another day.
Making beautiful water, we must have rain for water.)
Oh! We need more color. We need greens and pinks and
purples and reds. Let us make the earth and all the grasses
and flowers upon it. Who wants to be the earth? Now,
let's see here. We have the Sun, the Wind, the Grasses,
the Water, and now we need one more cloth. The sun
gives us light; therefore, we will end with the Night and
all the stars in the sky. So, this last piece of cloth is black
with yellow or white crystals in it, crystal-like patterns to
give the illusion of stars.

Once the people are
chosen, then the
storyteller begins to
pull out the cloths from
her goody-bag. The
first cloth in her goody-
bag is a bright-colored
red, yellow and black
square piece of cloth,
representing the sun.
Take out a cloth for
each of the elements
mentioned.

Now the rest of you out there in the audience, you are
going to have to help me too. Everyone look at me and
say this after me: "I am the tall mango tree." Raise your
hands up high. Wave your leaves.
"I am the flowing river." Let's flooooow. Move your
arms and hands so they flow like the all-mighty river.
"I am the morning sun."

Mime the action. For
the sun, storyteller lifts
hands to face and cups
hands underneath,
putting on a beautiful
smile.

Will you please say after me?
"I am the mountain high."
"I am the coooool breeze."
How does the breeze sound? Blow like the breeze.
(SHSHSHshiiiiiiiuuuuuu.)

"I am the STORYTELLER."

TUWAY TUWAY BARIMAH TUWAY TUWAY!
TUWAY TUWAY BARIMAH TUWAY TUWAY!

There was once a time in the forest when a very strange
thing happened: ALL   THE RAIN   JUST STOPPED
RAINING.
ALL   THE RIVERS   JUST STOPPED   FLOWING.

AND ALL   THE LAND   DRIED UP. (SHSHshiupp!)

There was no water. And the elements of nature became
very, very angry. The sun began to frown and growl
down at everyone. Okay, Sun. Stand up Let us see you
frown. And the wind began to blow fierce and scary.
Wind. Let us have you blow. (Shshiii.) And the water?
just disappeared. (Shshiuup! Bblbllllloooop.)

And the grasses began to ache and break, crack and dry up.
And the night was so lonely that all of the stars went
away.

The animals became very afraid and frightened. They
moaned and groaned; they needed water.

They moaned and groaned, Oooooaaah, ooooooaaah.
They walkwakwakwakwawawawalked and they
talktaktaktaktatatalked, and they moaned and groaned.
Oooooaah, Water. Water. They
walkwakwakwakwawawawalked and they

The storyteller lifts
her arms into a triangle
shape.
The storyteller lifts
her arms out and
wiggles her fingers to
give the illusion of the
breeze.

The storyteller has
everyone say this
together.

Open hands, imitating
falling rain

Suddenly change open
hands into fists, moving
arms and hands
backwards in a wave-
like motion, and then
abruptly stop.
Storyteller sucks in a
deep breath.

At this point, the
person who is playing
the Water will just lie
flatly down.
At this point, the
Night will walk off
stage, or the cloth will
be turned over so all you
can see is just the solid
part of it.
With mouth open and
hand to throat,
storyteller encourages
audience to moan and
groan.

talktaktaktaktatatalked, and they moaned and groaned. Ooooooah. Water.

The elephant sounded his trumpet, "Owooooooo!"

Mime action and make loud noise.

The gorilla pounded his drums: Bumbumbumbum BUMbumbumbum BUMbumbumbum BUMbumbumbum.

Mime action of drumming.

And then, all of a sudden out of the bush came the all-mighty Lion. "Achhaaau! Silence I say, silence. Now, look at yourselves. It is true we have no water. What are we going to do about it? Who has an idea?"

Loud, drawn-out roar. Imitate a lion by staring intently at audience and walking about.

Well, just then, over in the corner, an itsy-bitsy, teeny-weeny, litty-bitty chipmunk raised his hand . . . taptaptap . . . "Uh, King Lion. King Lion. I think we should all come together and dig for water."

Imitate timid chipmunk.

"Hummmm," said the Lion. "Excellent idea. That is what we all will do."

Now all of the animals agreed to dig for water except for one and that was the little lazy, tricky Sungura the Rabbit. "Agh! I'm too tired to dig for water. Later for you, folks." And Sungura the Rabbit hopped away. Hippityhoppity. Hippityhoppity Hippityhoppity. Hippityhoppity.

Hop about like a rabbit.

"Aaagh!" said the Lion. "I'll deal with that Sungura the Rabbit later. We're going to have to cooperate. We're going to have to work together. I want you to lift up your shovels and on the count of three, let's dig for water. Come on! One, two, three: Heave ho-ho, Heave ho-ho, Heave ho-ho, Heave ho-ho, Dig, Dig, Dig, Dig, Dig, Dig, Dig."

Audience mimes shoveling. Rhythm is long heave and short ho, ho.

"Wait a minute," said the Lion. "Silence. I think I've found something; it's cool, it's clear, it's clean, it's fresh, it's water! Come on! Drink it, drink it! Save yourselves. Wash your hands in it. Throw some on your faces. Yeeaay!"

Lion feels around in the "hole."

Audience follows directions.

At this point, the storyteller should say "Yeay" loud enough, or really with full emotion, so that the audience will know how to join in as well.

Oooh! Everyone was so happy. The sun began to smile. Let me see you smile, Sun! The wind began to smile. Oh! Let us see you smile, Wind. The water began to flow! Let us see you smile, Water. And the grasses began to grow. Oh, Grass. Let us see your beautiful smile. And the Night was so happy! All of the stars came back to the sky. TUWAY TUWAY BARIMAH TUWAY TUWAY! TUWAY TUWAY BARIMAH TUWAY TUWAY!

"However," said the King Lion, "It is true that we have our water back. But did everyone help us dig for it?"

"No!"

Audience responds.

"Who refused to help dig for the water?"

"Sungura the Rabbit!"

Audience responds.

"Yes, you are correct. Now, should we give Sungura the Rabbit some of our water?"

"Noooo!"

Audience responds.

"You are right, we shouldn't. And, do you know why? We need to teach him a lesson. But, we need someone to help us. Who among you out there can help us keep Sungura the Rabbit away?"

Yes! Thank you. Come here. What is your name, please? ["My name is Sarah."] [Sarah], have you ever seen a water buffalo before? ["No, I don't think I have."] Well, a water buffalo is an animal that lives in Kenya and it has a very special sound: Mmmmmuuuhhh. Something like a cow or a bull over in this country. [Sarah], I want you to use your imagination. and I want you to think how your water buffalo would sound. And, we're going to count to three and after we say, Three, I want you to give us the best, the biggest, moo sound you can. Okay? Are you ready? One, two, three . . . "Maawwwm." Beautiful! Beautiful! Let's clap for her! Beautiful. Okay, Water Buffalo, we are going to pretend that the water is right here. So you stand right here, right here at the water and don't move. No matter what happens, you stay right there.

Storyteller chooses a volunteer to be the water buffalo.

Walks water buffalo to waterhole.

Well, later that night, when all the stars were shining brightly, that tricky, lazy, sneaky Sungura the Rabbit came hopping up: "Tuway tuway Barimah tuway tuway. Tuway tuway Barimah tuway tuway." Tap tap tap tap. "Aaah, Hey, Water Buffalo, how ya doing Friend? Hey! It's me, Sungura the Rabbit. Hey, you know what? You looking good! Shake my hand. What you been up to? You know something, Water Buffalo? I got a present for you. Of course, I have. Put your hands together here. Now, Water Buffalo, I have brought you some delicious honey. The best honey in all of Kenya. Go ahead, go ahead, eat it, eat it. That's right, eat it." And while the water buffalo ate the honey, that tricky Sungura the Rabbit bent down and took some water. (SHshup, shshup, shshup, shshup.) "Humph Hah Huh Huh." And he hopped away.

Imitate a hopping rabbit.

Signal water buffalo away from the waterhole. As water buffalo drinks water, rabbit sneaks back to waterhole and drinks.

The next morning, the animals woke up, "Aaaaaah." They walked over to see the water buffalo. "Humph Hah Huh Huh. Buffalo, what have you been eating?"

Water buffalo answers storyteller's questions.

"Honey."

"Water Buffalo, who gave you this honey?"

"Sungura the Rabbit did."

"Uh oh, Water Buffalo. Did Sungura the Rabbit get any water?"

"Oh, I think so. Oh no."
But you did a beautiful job. Let's give her a nice hand. [Clap clap clap clap.]

Who can keep the Rabbit away? Who can keep Sungura away? Who can keep the Rabbit away? Who can keep Sungura away?

Oooh! Another volunteer. Come forward, please. What is your name, please? ["My name is Ricky."] [Ricky], have you ever seen a hyena before? ["Yes, I think I have."] Well, [Ricky], a hyena is an animal that comes from Kenya and is known for its crazy laughter HAHAHAhahahaaaah. Now [Ricky], you don't have to laugh like I just did. I want you to use your imagination. I want you to think back when you've been very happy, very excited about something and I want you to let all those giggles come bubbling out of you on the count of three. One, two, three, go. "Haaaaaaaah." Beautiful, beautiful! Let's give him a hand! [Clap clap clap.] Okay, Hyena. I want you to come and stand right here in front of the water and don't move, no matter what happens, you stand right there.

Well, later that night, all the stars were shining and twinkling brightly, and that lazy, tricky Sungura the Rabbit came hopping up: "Tuway tuway Barimah tuway tuway. Tuway tuway Barimah tuway tuway. Uh ahh. There is Hyena. He thinks he is so slick. But wait until he sees my trick." That sneaky Sungura the Rabbit went over to the grasses and he began to burrow in the grasses and the flowers, (shsh shsh shsh shsh shsh shsh shsh) and he began to throw them on his head until he had a nice blanket and he began to dance around the hyena. "Tuway tuway Barimah tuway tuway. Tuway tuway Barimah tuway tuway." And slowly, Sungura the Rabbit began to wrap the hyena around and around and around in the blanket until the hyena could not move. At that point, Sungura the Rabbit bent down and took some water. (Shshup shshup shshup shshup.) "Hahahaha hahahaha hahahaha hahaaaaaaa."

The next morning, the animals woke up, "Aahhh." Let's wake up like the animals everybody, "Aaaahhhhhh."
They walked over to the hyena, "Hmph, hmph, hmph."

"Oh, Hyena! Hyena! Where are you?"

Water buffalo leaves the stage.

Storyteller chooses a volunteer to be the hyena.

Walks the hyena to the waterhole.

Mime the action. Or, taking a large piece of cloth, wrap it around the entire body of the hyena while they're standing up.

Audience responds.

"Hehehehehehehe"

"Hyena, is that you?"

"Hehehehehehehe"

"What's the matter? Who wraped you up like this?"

"Sungura the Rabbit did."

"Oh no, Hyena.

Did Sungura the Rabbit get any of the water?"

"Yes, I'm afraid so."

"Oh, Sungura. Oh, that naughty Sungura. But never mind, Hyena. We will help you out." Let's see here: Tuway tuway Barimah tuway tuway. Tuway tuway Barimah tuway tuway. Does the hyena have any friends out there?

Oh, let's give the hyena a big hand! Thank you. You may be seated.

Who can keep the Rabbit away? Who can keep Sungura away? Who can keep the Rabbit away? Who can keep Sungura away?

Oooh, I see a volunteer. Come up, please. Yes, what is your name? ["My name is Mary."] [Mary], have you ever seen a turtle before? ["Yes."] Well, let's talk about the turtle. What's special about a turtle? What does a turtle have on its back? ["A shell."] Very good. Now, how does a turtle move? Does a turtle move fast or does a turtle move slowly? ["Slowly."] Well, [Mary,] I want you to use your imagination, and on the count of three, I want you to walk very slowly for us. One, two, three. Tu-way-tu-way-Ba-ri-mah-tu-way-tu-way. Tu-way-tu-way-Ba-ri-mah-tu-way-tu-way. Beautiful. Let's give her a hand. Now [Mary], I want you to use your imagination again and I want you to pretend you see a big tall beautiful tree. Look up high. Lift your head. Do you see that tall beautiful tree? Good. Now I want you to take your fingers and I want you to shake and wiggle your fingers. That's right. Shake and wiggle your fingers, and you are going to take some sap from the tree. Do you know what sap is? Well, sap is very sticky—sticky like syrup. Let's get lots of sap and I want you to rub it on your shell. That's right. Put it all over your back. Very good. Now the tree has disappeared and we are going to slowly walk over to the water. Tuway tuway Barimah tuway tuway. Tuway tuway Barimah tuway tuway. Okay, Turtle, I want you to slowly bend down on the floor and I want you to fold your arms and stick your head inside your shell. That's right, Turtle. And you wait right there and don't move. I want you to be very, very still so that when that tricky little Rabbit pops up, here's what's going to happen.

Storyteller sings the song while untying the hyena, or ask for someone from the audience to come up and untie the hyena.

Hyena leaves the stage.

Storyteller chooses a volunteer to be the turtle.

The two walk slowly over to the tree. Storyteller touches the imaginary sap. Opens and closes index finger and thumb to indicate its stickiness. Guides turtle's hand to the sap and helps to put some all over the turtle's back. Walk together back to the waterhole.

Turtle bends down on knees. Storyteller whispers in turtle's ear.

Well, later that night when the stars were out shining and twinkling brightly, that lazy, tricky Sungura the Rabbit came hopping up: "Tuay tuway Barimah tuway tuway. Hah hah hah hah! Tuay tuway Barimah tuway tuway. Hah hah hah. Why look, there's nobody here! The water is all mine. There is even a smooth stone I can step on. And, you know what! This stone is so shiny, I'm going to sit on this stone and I'm going to drink all the water I want."

Rabbit hops over to smooth stone.

So, what the rabbit didn't realize is that the smooth stone is really *what*?
"The turtle's shell."
And the turtle's shell had what on its back?
"Sap."
And sap is very *what*?
"Sticky."

Storyteller asks audience.

Audience responds.

So, when Sungura the Rabbit began to bend down and touch what he thought was a smooth stone, his hands became very stuck.

Rabbit's hands get stuck on Turtle's back (place hands on the turtle's back and sway back and forth).

"Heeelp! Help! Help! Let me go, let me go, let me go, I can't move. Help! Let me go."

And the turtle rose up out of the water; she lifted out her arms and she lifted her head and she said, in a very proud way: "I caught the Rabbit." Yeay! Let's give her a hand. Yeay!

Storyteller signals the turtle to stand up, and motions the turtle to spread out arms, lift up head and look proud.

Now Sungura the Rabbit feels so bad about what he has done that he promises never to do it again. And there is a saying that Sungura the Rabbit says that has traveled all around the world and back again, and that is, "You don't miss your water until your well runs dry."

Let's give everyone who helped in the story of Sungura a big hand. Thank you.

NOTES

Background Information

Most people have heard of Bugs Bunny. Some people have heard of Brer Rabbit, and fewer still have heard of Sungura the Rabbit and Kalulu the Rabbit, who come out of Africa. Actually, the Rabbit Stories or the Rabbit out of Africa are the great greatgreatgreatgreatgreatgreatgreatgrandfather of Brer Rabbit and Bugs Bunny.

The rabbit character is a trickster because the rabbit character uses his cunning, his wit, or his instinct to get him in and out of trouble. Most of the stories that are told about Brer Rabbit, Bugs Bunny or Sungura or Kalulu the Rabbit out of Africa, show

how the rabbit uses his trickery and outwits a larger animal, usually the lion or the water buffalo. But sometimes, as it is true in life, even the rabbit must learn his lesson. So this story, "Sungura the Rabbit," is the type of story that shows no matter how tricky the rabbit is, he too must get caught and learns his lesson.

In the Afro-American tradition, Brer Rabbit is caught in pretty much the same way Sungura the Rabbit is caught. The Tar Baby Story is a very popular story that was told down South. As a matter of fact, I heard this story when I was a young child growing up in Alcoa, Tennessee. Once I went to college and began to study folklore and collect stories, I was amazed to find stories from Kenya and from other parts of Africa similar to the Tar Baby Story. Brer Rabbit, as with Sungura and Kalulu, and even Bugs Bunny, is a trickster type who uses his wit and his cunning to get in and out of all kinds of situations. Brer Rabbit and Sungura are survivors—Brer Rabbit escaped out of slavery. He showed black people that we couldn't rely on magic. Even though we might escape or we might get caught, we could learn from this and we were to keep trying.

The cloths that are used in the story do not necessarily have to be African cloth. They can be any type of cloth that attracts the storyteller who is using the story. In other words, you can get these cloths from J. C. Penny's, Woolworth's or from your home; they may be from an old sheet or an old curtain. Anything that looks like an element of nature to you will do. The elements of nature can vary; sometimes I add the sky or sometimes I add mountains. You can have seven pieces of cloth or you can have five pieces of cloth; it doesn't matter. The whole idea of how I tell the story and why I tell the story is to involve the audience; but it is up to the storyteller, or the person who is choosing to tell the story, to tell it in a way that naturally involves the audience. Even when you ask for volunteers from the audience, it should be done in a very casual or in a very exciting way, so that everyone wants to participate. This story is designed to wake up the imagination, to shock the senses, and to get everybody involved. That is why it is very important when I say, "Yeay!" after the water has been found again that everyone naturally joins in with me with that "Yeay!"

Related Books

AFRICAN MYTHS AND TALES, edited by Susan Feldman. New York. Dell Press. 1977.

THE DAY WHEN THE ANIMALS TALKED, by William J. Faulkner. Chicago. Follet Press. 1977. A marvelous collection of Brer Rabbit tales.

SUNGURA, (stories) adapted by Mae Turner Reggy. Washington, D.C. Alrag Productions. 1973. Two amusing moral stories about Sungura the Rabbit from Kenya.

"Warriors to Rabbits: Collecting Stories in Kenya," by Heather McNeil McQuarie from *The Storytelling Journal*. (Jonesborough, TN: NAPPS, 1988), vol. 5, no. 2: pp. 31-33. Ms. McQuaire recounts her trip to Kenya and how she collected fifty stories from various tribes. Several of the stories were about Rabbit.

WHERE LEPOARD PASSES (1968) and THE LONG GRASS WHISPERS (l968), by Geraldine Eliot. New York. Schocken Books. Stories from the Ngoni people in Africa. Rabbit is called Kalulu.

WHO'S IN RABBIT'S HOUSE, adapted by Vera Aardema. New York. Dial Press. 1977. A rabbit story from Kenya beautifully illustrated and well written.

WORLD TALES FOR CREATIVE DRAMATICS AND STORYTELLING, edited by Burdette S. Fitzgerald. Prentice-Hall, Inc. 1962. This collection includes a wonderful tale from the

Afro-American tradition titled "The Rabbit that Wouldn't Help Dig aWell," edited by George W. Caldwell, which was originally published in the *Journal of American Folklore* in l934. This version is similiar to "The Rabbit at the Waterhole," except for the ending, which concludes with the trickster rabbit escaping unharmed.

"Tar Baby," a traditional tale about Brer Rabbit from the South, can be found in most anthologies of Afro-American folklore, such as *The Book of Negro Folklore*, edited by Langston Hughes and Arna Bontemp (Dodd Mead, 1958).

ADAPTED BY
BILL HARLEY

The Freedom Bird

NARRATIVE

In this story from Thailand, the bird's song is the Thai equivalent of a common taunt you probably heard children use sometime or other. You know the one, "You can't catch me—na na nana naaaa!" Now if YOU will be the sassy bird, this story will be a lot more fun. Want to try the bird song one time?

Storyteller gives taunt as he/she wishes it to be uttered, then motions for audience to repeat the taunt.

And after the taunt, you clap three times, like this.

And the clap.

And hey, if you feel like letting loose with childish gestures of defiance—you know, like thumbing your nose, or WHATEVER!—this is your big opportunity!

Lead audience in taunt and claps, repeating twice.

Once upon a time, there was a hunter. He hunted with a bow and arrow and, one day, he decided he wanted to go hunting in the woods. So he took his quiver of arrows, put them on his shoulder, and he took his bow and he headed off, into the woods . . . deep, deep, deeper than he had ever been before. And when he got WAY back in the woods, he heard a song he had never heard in the woods before. NA NA NANA NA.

Lead chant of taunt and three sharp claps.

"What's that song?" he growled. "I don't like it!" And he headed deeper and deeper into the woods until he came to one special tree, and he looked up into that tree, and there, at the top of that tree, he saw a very small golden bird, the most beautiful bird he'd seen in his entire life. And the bird looked down at him and said . . .

NA NA NA etc., with three sharp hand claps.

And he said, "How can such a beautiful bird as you have such an ugly voice?" And the bird said . . .

NA NA NA etc., with three sharp hand claps.

The hunter said, "Oh, yeah? Well, I'll teach you a lesson!" And he reached into his quiver and he pulled out an arrow and he put the arrow in the bow and he pulled back the string—whoosh!

The storyteller may mime activity as he shoots arrow.

The arrow headed straight for the bird, but the bird saw it coming, hopped to the next branch, and the arrow went right past. The bird looked down at the hunter and said. . .

NA NA NA etc., with three sharp hand claps.

"Oh, yeah?" said the hunter. "Well, I'll get you this time!" And he pulled another arrow out of his quiver, put it in the bow, pulled back the string, let go—whoosh! That arrow headed straight for the bird, but this time the bird didn't see it coming and [one clap] it went right through the bird's heart. The bird fell off the branch, fell through the leaves of the tree, and as it fell to the ground, the hunter caught that bird in his sack, threw the sack over his shoulder, and started to walk home. When he was almost home, he heard some sounds coming out of that sack!

"What!!" he said. He got home, put the sack down. He reached into the sack, pulled out that bird. He looked at it and put it on the kitchen counter and pulled all the feathers off!

Storyteller muffles taunt and three sharp hand claps, twice.

Storyteller makes sound of pulling off each feather as he mimes the activity. Put-put-put-put-put-put, etc.

"Ahhh!" he said with a sound of relief. He turned around, and as he turned around, he heard . . .

Storyteller leads audience in muffled TAUNT/CLAPS with closed lips.

"Ohh, no!" he said. "What's that?" He looked at that bird, then he reached for the biggest knife he could find, and he CHOPPED that bird into a hundred small pieces. Chop, chop, chop, chop, chop, chop, chop, chop.

Then he washed the knife, turned around to put it away, and he heard . . .

Storyteller chops very, very fast with voice and arm motions.

TAUNT/CLAPS with "Chop" instead of "Na."

"Oh, no!" He walked over to that bird all in pieces with a huge pot full of water, scraped every last piece into the pot and put it on the stove. Then he turned up the flame under the pot—high, as high as it could go. Pretty soon, the water started to roll, and bubble, and he pushed all those pieces down into the boiling pot. But the minute his back was to the pot, he heard . . . burgh, burgh, burgh, burgh, burgh, burgh, burgh!

Storyteller introduces gurgling sounds for audience to mimic with same TAUNT/CLAPS.

"I don't believe this!!" He grabbed that pot, he ran out into the yard, he got a shovel, he started to dig a deep, deep hole in the ground. When the hole was way over his head, he climbed out and poured all the parts of the bird into the hole and covered it up with dirt. And he stamped on it. "HAA!" He breathed a big sigh of relief and started back to the house. He was just about to open the door to go inside when he heard, from deep down in the ground . . . Nah, nah, nah, nah, nah, nah, nah, nah!

Storyteller holds hand over mouth to be sure TAUNT/CLAPS are heavily muffled.

OH NO! OH NO! Now the hunter was more furious than he'd ever been in his life! He ran back, he grabbed his shovel and dug up every last piece of that bird and put them in a little wooden box. He put a top on that box, then he got a huge rock and tied it on top of the box with some heavy rope. Then he went down to the river and FLUNG the box as far as he could, out into the water. And he watched as the box splashed and sank. And he stood on the banks and listened, [long pause] and he didn't hear a thing. So he walked home.

Now that box stayed at the bottom of the river for two days. And the current of the water rushing down to the sea began to push that rock back and forth, back and forth, and the rope loosened, and loosened, until, one day, the rock fell off. The box was made of wood, so it floated to the top of the river and started to float downstream for one, two, then three days. On the third day, the box floated by some children who were playing by the banks of the river. They saw that box and wondered what was in it. One of them waded out into the river and as the box floated by, she caught it! And she walked back to the shore, put the box down, and everyone looked at it. Then she reached down and pulled the top off. As soon as the box was opened, 100 golden birds flew out and they were all singing in a full voice.

Storyteller leads audience in triumphant TAUNT/CLAPS.

Well, about a year later, that same hunter was walking through the same woods. Far off in the distance, he heard a song he thought he had heard before.

TAUNT/CLAPS.

"OH NO! NOT AGAIN!" he said. He walked and walked and walked until he came to the same tree he'd been under a year before, and where, before, he had seen only one golden bird, he now saw 100 golden birds, all looking down at him, and singing out. [to audience] Can you sound like 100 birds now?

Really loud TAUNT/CLAPS.

The hunter scratched his head, looked up at all those birds, thought and thought—finally said, "Why has it taken me so long to realize this? I should have known from the very beginning. I know who you are. You're the freedom bird. Freedom can't be killed off. We just have to let you *be!*" And all those birds looked down at the hunter and sang out to him, at the top of their lungs.

TAUNT/CLAPS.

And that's the story of the Freedom Bird.

NOTES

This story was brought back from Chang Mi, Thailand by David Holt, who heard it told in broken English by, one of his guides, a 10 year old boy. David set it down on paper, worked with it and came up this tale that Bill Harley recorded on his tape, *Monsters in the Bathroom*.

David Holt's tours of India, Thailand, Burma, Bolivia and Columbia for the U. S. State Department have introduced world audiences to traditional American music, dance, and mountain tales. The Columbian newspaper *El Mundo* said of David, "He was a better ambassador than the Peace Corps, foreign aid and all the diplomats put together." Never underestimate the power of the storyteller!

Juan Bobo and Sisi

NARRATIVE

AUDIENCE RESPONSE OR TELLER'S ACTION

I am a storyteller. I have no pictures to show you or books to read. I have only my words, movements, and songs. You, however, have your mind's eye to create even better pictures than the ones in books. From time to time, I will ask one of you to tell us the picture you have created in your mind's eye. I want to give as many of you as possible a chance to share. Everyone can share pictures by drawing them later.

Storyteller mimes opening a book by holding hands in a prayer position and opening them as if they were a book. Then mime turning pages with one hand.

In my story, which takes place on the island of Puerto Rico, we will be singing a traditional folk song from the West Indies called "The Mango Walk." Let's practice it a bit. [See the Notes following story.]

My mother she done tell me that you go mango walk, you go mango walk, you go mango walk.
My mother she done tell me that you go mango walk and steal all the number 'leven.

Storyteller leads in singing the song two or three times. This part can be omitted if time is short.

In Puerto Rico, storytellers often begin their stories by saying, "Once upon a time, or two, or three." I will begin this way also. Once upon a time, or two, or three, on the island of Puerto Rico, there lived a boy named Juan Bobo. He was [age] years old. Juan Bobo had a very special friend and pet named SiSi. SiSi wasn't an ordinary pet, as you may have. SiSi was special. She was a chicken.

Substitute any age which seems appropriate for the group before you.

Put hands on waist with elbows bent. Move elbows forward and backward, with knees bent. Scratch feet against the ground while you stretch your head forward and back like a chicken. Chicken sounds are made by covering teeth with firm lips, and then using nasal, high voice to say, "Bahk "(pause), "Bahk/Bahk" (quickly together), "Bahk," and repeat.

They lived in a barrio with Juan Bobo's mother, who couldn't afford many toys, so Juan Bobo and SiSi played together often. What games do you think they might play together on the island of Puerto Rico, where it is so sunny, so green with palm trees, and so hot? Close your eyes and feel the sun, and see Juan Bobo and SiSi playing together. [Example: Yes, you're right! SiSi LOVED soccer. You wouldn't think that a chicken bird would have a strong head but *she* did! She always sent the ball flying!]

Invite responses from several children. Expect to hear, "they played hide and seek," "soccer," "hiding in the bathtub," or "checkers!" Reply "Yes, you're right!" to each, and elaborate on each fantasy a little with words and/or pantomime.

As you can see, SiSi was a special chicken—a very special chicken bird. She even liked to listen to Juan Bobo play the bongo drums and sing "The Mango Walk." That was her favorite time of the day.

One day, she actually got right up and did a little chicken dance to the song. From that day on, everyone in the barrio enjoyed watching SiSi do her Chicken Mango Walk dance. You sing it with me while I show you her chicken dance. Everyone can play the bongo drums on their knees like this.

> My mother she done tell me that you go mango walk,
> you go mango walk, you go mango walk.
> My mother she done tell me that you go mango walk
> and steal all the number 'leven.

Demonstrate on real bongos or with your hands on knees. Keep the rhythm of "The Mango Walk" by striking the knee or drum to the rhythm of the words. You can alternate knees as you would the drums. Be sure hand is raised high overhead after "Ole!" The audience plays and sings too.

That's wonderful. Now, on the count of THREE, you all start playing and I will show you SiSi's Chicken Mango Walk. One, Two, Three.

Step on toes from side to side to the rhythm of the words quickly and lightly. Hold thumbs under armpits with bent elbows and flap them also to the rhythm of the words. On the words "Ole!"

turn around and wiggle the buttocks to end the dance. This always brings a good laugh.

Well, not many months went by before a stranger appeared on the edge of the barrio where Juan Bobo lived. This stranger had a big hat and a very big mustache. As a matter of fact, that mustache, which he curled up, would stre-e-etch from one arm to the other if straightened out.

Mime curled mustache with circular motion of index finger next to upper lip. For "straightened," uncurl and hold arm out at shoulder level.

The stranger had been watching SiSi dance. When she was finished, the stranger said, "Juan Bobo, come over here. I have something to tell you. I would like to *buy* your SiSi bird and take her to the marketplace to have her dance for people who will pay *me* money."

Use a lower register, slower pacing, for stranger's voice.

Stress "buy" and "me."

The stranger held out fifty dollars for Juan Bobo. Juan's mouth dropped open in surprise. He had never seen so much money. "Why, I could buy my mother a Christmas present, a birthday present, and even have money for myself!" He thought about what all that money could buy. All of a sudden, he realized if he took the money, SiSi would never be his again. So he told the man, "NO! She is not for sale!" The stranger left and Juan Bobo went back to play with SiSi.

Hold out your hand.

Drop your mouth.

Look up, as if you are "thinking hard."

Quicken voice on "All of a sudden."

But SiSi had overheard, and she saw how Juan Bobo had looked at that money. She was hurt and angry. So she went on a hunger strike! A hunger strike! She wouldn't eat a thing. Not corn, not seed. She would not eat a thing a chicken is supposed to eat. She was hurt and angry.

And so passed una, dos, tres, quatro, cinco, seis, siete dias. Seven days. But the chicken refused to eat.

Students usually begin to count with me spontaneously as I hold up my fingers for each day ("dias" means "days").

Poor Juan. Can you imagine how he felt, looking at his poor skinny bird? He tried so hard to get her to eat. He offered her everything she used to enjoy. She refused. He offered her everything *he* enjoyed—pizza, steak, MacDonald's hamburgers, strawberry sundaes. She refused. He offered her everything *you* enjoy. What do *you* love eating?

To everything offered say, "Yes, he tried that, too. She refused." Even if an item is repeated, say, "Yes, but she just lifted up her head and said 'Bahk,' which means 'No' in chicken talk."

25

Finally, Juan Bobo said to SiSi, "Will you eat if I promise to take you to the marketplace myself? Oh, it is so exciting there! I will show you everything, and I myself will let you dance for all the people, is that what you want to do?"

SiSi began to eat again. When she got all her strength back, Juan Bobo walked with her to the market. Oh, they had many adventures on the way to the market. Now, use your mind's eye, tell me what *you* saw happening on the way to the market, one at a time.

Do the SiSi walk with happy face, nodding head up and down for "Yes, Yes." (See directions, above.)

Expect to hear about a snake, or a rabbit. Respond: "Yes, you're right, they met a rabbit who taught them how to hop." (or) "Yes, you're right, they met a snake who frightened them with his hiss. Juan Bobo started to play his bongos. The snake loved it and forgot his meanness." etc.

All of a sudden it started to rain. If you listen very carefully, you will hear what it sounded like. Do what I do and keep it going until I change your movement. At the end I will give this signal to stop. First, rub your hands together. Now, snap your fingers softly. Now clap—but softly. Now slap your thighs as hard as you can. Oh, that rain has become a STORM.

Demonstrate an ending signal. I use a conductor's ending signal, which is like a breaststroke movement of the arms.

Juan Bobo and SiSi ran and ran till Juan Bobo saw a cave. They ran inside the cave out of the storm. It was *quiet* inside the cave. It was a big cave—and dark.

Mime running. Remain in place and lift heels off floor rapidly with knees bent. Move arms, elbows bent, as though running.

Emphasize "quiet" by a crossing movement of hands.

Juan Bobo's mind was fixed on the outside of the cave because he was close enough to see the rain falling. SiSi became curious and wandered further into the cave. When Juan Bobo realized she was gone, he began to feel his way into the deep, dark cavern.

To "feel your way," use classical mime action called "the wall." Cup your hands, palms facing out in front of face, elbows bent. Press one hand flat against an imaginary wall. Then press the other hand flat. Relax the first hand into the shape of a cup and press it flat against another place on the wall.

All of a sudden, Juan Bobo knew that he and SiSi were not alone in that cave! "Oh, SiSi. We're not alone here!" Use your mind's eye to see what he saw. What scary creature did he see in the cave? Tell me what you see there.

Demonstrate his fear by shaking your knees.

Expect to hear "a dragon," "a monster," and "a bear" among others. For example, "That cave creature had a bear's body and it was green, with hair all over, a tail like a dragon's. It had one eye and it sounded just like a robot!" Shake knees as you say this. Shake them from side to side. Keep them a little bent.

Yes, yes—that's what he saw! It was strange. "Let's get out of here," said Juan Bobo.

Just then Juan Bobo heard a squawking sound as the cave creature rushed by and actually brushed against him. The cave creature was carrying SiSi under its arm. It was carrying SiSi away! Juan Bobo ran after it saying, "Stop, thief, stop! You can't take SiSi! She's my best friend!"

Mime running after thief (see directions above). Voice ends in a cry.

Juan Bobo ran and ran but he couldn't catch the cave creature. He had to stop because the pain in his side hurt so much. He watched the cave creature grow smaller and smaller as it ran. "That creature is like none I've ever seen before. It belongs in a *zoo!*"

Juan Bobo went back to the barrio feeling a great loss. His friends were concerned and said they would help him find SiSi. So they began to think of plans of action to capture the weird-looking cave creature. Juan Bobo explained, "It should be brought to the zoo people because it is so very different from other creatures." The friends agreed. What do you think they decided to do?

Listen to several plans. Say "You're right! One friend brought a rope." "You're right! Another friend made a big cage," etc. If a child says, "They got a gun to shoot him dead," you can say that's exactly what one friend said but then she remembered their decision about the zoo. You can also make the gun a tranquilizer gun. Use three or four ideas in a combined plan.

After the plans were made, Juan Bobo went to the sheriff and suggested the BIG plan. He said, "We can bring rope, [list all the items]. "Good idea," said the sheriff.

And so Juan Bobo and his friends brought the ropes, [etc]. When they arrived, they felt their way into the deep, dark recesses of the cave. They set the traps and waited. Finally they heard the cave creature galumphing along. Galumph, galumph, galumph. When the creature was close enough all the friends let go of the ropes [etc.].

Mime moving along the wall. (See directions above.)

Draw out the "galumphs" so that the footsteps seem long and heavy. Use the top of your body to emphasize weight sinking on each "galumph."

Storyteller can invite several listeners to participate in pantomiming the actions.

They caught the cave creature in their traps and made sure he was tied up tight. Just as they did, they looked at the cave creature and couldn't believe their eyes. Its head had come off. "Eeeeeeew!" "Uck." "Ugh. . . ." Everyone expected to see blood and veins. Instead, when they peeked inside the cave creature's neck they saw a big MUSTACHE.

Make an appropriately disgusted face.

"Wait a minute. I've seen that mustache before. Why, that's not a cave creature; that's the stranger!" said Juan Bobo.

The sheriff pulled out a poster he had removed from the wall of his office—on a hunch. Sure enough, the man in that WANTED picture with a mustache was in the cave creature's neck!

"Juan Bobo, you have helped to capture the most wanted thief in all of Puerto Rico! And do you know what?" asked the sheriff. "There is a reward for his capture."

You can use your mind's eye. What do you think the reward turned out to be? You're right! He received [a medal, etc.]. What else did he receive?

Accept all answers as part of the reward. I stop at two or three. Usually one of the answers is money.

Juan Bobo knew that now he could buy his mother a birthday present, a Christmas present and he still had SiSi. You know, if it weren't for SiSi, he and his friends would never have captured the thief in the first place. Right then and there, Juan Bobo decided to have a big fiesta in honor of SiSi.

"I will put you up on a pedestal and you can dance the Mango Walk. But this time we shall call it the 'SiSi Walk.' "

And that's just what they did. They had a big fiesta and all his friends took turns learning to dance the SiSi Walk while Juan Bobo and the others played the drums with their hands and knees. Now some of you can practice the SiSi Walk with me up here while the rest of you will play the drums with your knees and sing.

And that my friends is the story of Juan Bobo and SiSi!

If no one mentions money I simply say Juan Bobo decided to have a fiesta in honor of SiSi.

I invite six to eight students to dance the SiSi Walk. (See directions above for dance.) I also give several instruments to a few children. Maracas, drums, and steel drums are favorites. These children keep the rhythm of "The SiSi Walk!"

NOTES

There is a story called "Ladrillo and the Hen," recorded by Reinaldo and Ana Matos in the booklet *Ladrillo and Tales of Juan Bobo: Puerto Rican Folk Tales*, published by the Connecticut Program for Migrant Children, Hartford, Ct., 1973. The story I call "Juan Bobo and SiSi" uses the traditional folk character Juan Bobo but differs in most other respects. The hen is not a "character" in the Matos version and Ladrillo has become a thief in the disguise of a cave creature in the present version I created. Also, the present version uses song, dance, instruments, a sheriff, and continues to grow with each new audience. The audience helps to nourish the plot each time I tell it. That's how the chicken grew into a real character. I noticed the children's eyes and their increased interest the first time I described SiSi and showed how she walked. Her character grew from that point on and the story truly became a story of the "folk."

I encourage my graduate students to use fantasies by improvising verbally and nonverbally on what they receive. You might want to do the same. If you do choose to improvise and find yourself with an interesting version, please contact me; they may well find their way into my new book, *Organic Storytelling*.

I developed the "organic" style from watching my friend, storyteller Mara Capy, tell stories using an African style of telling in which an audience member might say at any point in the narration, "Storyteller, I was present." The teller pauses and says, "And what did you see, my child [or woman, etc.]?" The listener then tells her or his version and then the teller validates the listener by saying, "Ah, for sure my child, you were there!" The teller then integrates the listener's vision into the story by improvising during the next part of the story.

I simply adapted the method to meet the needs of audiences in the northeastern part of the United States where students in assemblies are not always a real community, ready to share time and space as well as some other audiences might. In assemblies of 50-250 students, I tell the listeners that I will ask them from time to time about the pictures in their mind's eye. When I ask them to create a picture they can let me know that they have one by raising their hand. Then, at the time, I point to one person, listen to their "picture" and use whatever they give me, always validating their response with, "You're right!" There is always at least one student who will turn to another, joyfully giggle and say, "I'm right!" This may be the only time that student has been right all day, or even all week! And in front of all these people too! Creatively gifted students also benefit from this approach. They can create on their own levels, giving detailed scientific or wildly creative ideas.

Telling a story "organically" is a thrilling experience for the teller as well as the listener. I encourage you to try it!

THE MANGO WALK

1. My moth-er she done tell me that you go Man-go walk, you go Man-go walk, you go. Man-go walk. My moth-er she done tell me that you go Man-go walk and steal'all the num-ber 'lev-en. Oh, Cay!

Note: When you steal all the numbers 'leven you have all the luck that the number 'eleven brings. You are lucky!

Williwu, the Lonely Little Witchgirl

Introduction

There are two ways in which "Williwu" can be told. Both ways the audience is informed beforehand that there is a refrain that Williwu hears throughout the story. The storyteller chants or sings it, and then teaches it. The audience is requested to chant or sing the refrain when it's time, as follows:

"It's up to you, Williwu,
This is something you must do,
If you don't do it very soon,
You won't make it to the moon."

If the storyteller prefers to have the above refrain sung by the audience, there is music to accompany this rhyme (see Notes). Either way—chanting or singing—the tale is greatly enhanced by having the audience be Williwu's prompter. A second way that works well with children is to encourage them to join in whenever there are repetitions, which occur frequently throughout the story.

At the very end of the story, more excitement and delight can be aroused by teaching the audience a song (see Notes). This is optional. An original dance of the storyteller's creation can also be taught to accompany this song.

NARRATIVE

AUDIENCE RESPONSE
OR TELLER'S ACTION

Long, long ago, next to the Cahokia Mounds [or insert name of local area] stood a little house in which lived seven little witchgirls. Six of them were perfect toughies. They fought all day and went around doing as much mischief as they possibly could. But the seventh one, whose name was WILLIWU, was different.

No matter how hard she tried, Williwu could not manage to be bad. That caused a lot of trouble between her and her witchgirl cousins. They had been taught by all the old witches that being good was the same as being stupid. And who wants to be stupid? Not those little witchgirls! So they despised Williwu. They played tricks on her, they called her horrible names, they tripped her while she walked, laughed at her—and who do you suppose was forced to do all the dirty work around the house? WILLIWU!

Wait only briefly for a reply, and then go on.

Poor Williwu—with no one to talk to—she was a lonely little witchgirl.

One bright Halloween Day, the witchgirls told Williwu to get their flying brooms out of the closet and dust them off for their trip to the moon. This was a big event, in fact the most important and most wonderful thing they did all year. On the night of October 31st, without fail, at midnight, all the little witches and the big witches mounted their flying brooms and were off to the moon for a big party. (Some day I shall tell you about that party, but right now I want to tell you what happened that morning to Williwu.)

No sooner did she open the closet door than hundreds of little house mice scampered out, and Williwu saw they had eaten all the branches off the brooms. They had left only tiny little stubs! And that wasn't all they did! The broom*sticks* were full of little toothmarks where the mice had tried to bite into the wood too! These brooms could take no witch anywhere! These brooms could not even fly as high as the housetop—and they would surely NEVER make the moon!

Williwu called her cousins over and when they saw what had happened, they began to wail and scream and screech most horribly!

At this point storyteller asks audience to tell her/him how this might sound.

Only Williwu stayed calm. "Why don't we go to the witchbroom maker," said Williwu, "and buy seven new brooms?" For once, the cousins did not make fun of her idea. They dashed off to the witchbroom maker's house, yelling:

> "Witchbroom maker, Witchbroom maker, QUICK! QUICK!
> Sell us each a broom, so we can fly to the moon."

But the witchbroom maker said, "I'm sorry, I have only six brooms left. One of you will have to stay home tonight."

"Let it be Williwu," screamed the six witchgirls wickedly, and before the witchbroom maker could stop them, they pushed him aside, stormed into his shop, grabbed the six brooms and flew away.

"Come back, you little brats!" cried the witchbroom maker furiously. "You didn't even pay! I never saw naughtier witchgirls than you!" And then shaking his fist at them far up in the sky by now, he said, "If ever I get my hands on you, I'll give you knuckleheads instead of brooms."

"Oh!" he stormed to himself as he went back inside and shut the door, "I HATE TO BE TREATED LIKE THAT!"

All of a sudden he noticed that not all the witchgirls had left. One was still standing inside his house, off in a corner, and her eyes were filled with tears.

"What are you doing here?" snarled the broommaker. "Are you waiting for a knucklehead?"

"No, I get plenty of those from my cousins," cried the girl. "I am Williwu, and I stayed here because I hate to go home. My witch cousins will laugh at me all afternoon for not having a broom to fly to the moon."

"That's the nastiest bunch of witchgirls I ever saw!" said the witchbroom maker. "You seem to be much nicer."

"That's my problem," wailed Williwu. "I simply can not manage to be bad. Sometimes I wonder if I really am a witchgirl. I never do anything the way I'm supposed to. But this is the worst thing that has ever happened to me, because any witch or witchgirl who doesn't make it to the moon on Halloween night will be the laughingstock of all the other witches forever and ever."

"I know how you feel," said the witchbroom maker. "To be laughed at hurts more than being scolded. I know because kids used to make fun of me, too. As you can see, my legs are a little crooked, so I can't run like other people."

When Williwu looked down at them, drying off her tears, she saw that his legs were more than a *little* crooked. They were *very* crooked. But she was too polite to say anything, and the witchbroom maker went on. "Let me see, maybe I can help you so those hooligans can't make fun of you for not getting to the moon. You'll have to be real quick, though. Run to the willow tree and ask him to give you an armful of branches. I think I have just enough time to make a very fine broom, so you can fly to the moon."

The witchbroom maker expected Williwu to be delighted at the very idea, but Williwu was not used to kindness. She was also frightened. She said,

> "Oh, gee, I don't even know the willow tree.
> Please—would you come along with me?"

"I can't," said the kind old witchbroom maker. "You know I can't run. We'd never make it in time."

And then he said, slowly and clearly. . . [to audience]. . .

Can you guess what he said? [Don't wait for words. Lead audience to say with you:]

Storyteller pauses significantly to alert audience.

Motion to audience to chant the refrain

> "It's up to *you*, Williwu,
> This is something you must do,
> If you don't do it very soon
> You'll never make it to the moon."

"All right, I'll try," said Williwu with a sigh. She took a deep breath and ran all the way to the willow tree. When she got there, she said, all out of breath and in a rush, "Willow tree, dear willow tree, I am Williwu, the little witchgirl. Would you please give me some branches so I can take them to the witchbroom maker? He promised to make a broom so I can fly to the moon."

In a weak little voice, the willow tree replied, "I wish I could, but look at me! Ever since the well stopped sending me water, my branches stopped growing. My roots are so dry, I think I'm about to die.

"Would you run to the well and ask him to send me some water? If I got some water, I could give you some branches to take to the witchbroom maker. I am sure he could make you a fine broom so you could fly to the moon."

"Oh, dear," said Williwu, "I don't know how to talk to the well. I wish someone could come along with me."

"I can't move, as you can see," said the sad old willow tree. And then Williwu heard those words again.

She wasn't sure whether the willow tree said them, or whether they came to her from the air, but all the same, *she heard them*. [Ask audience] What did she hear?

> "It's up to *you*, Williwu,
> This is something *you* must do,
> If you don't do it very soon,
> You'll never make it to the moon."

"All right, I'll try," said Williwu with a sigh. She took a deep breath and ran all the way to the well. When she got there, she said, "Dear well, I am Williwu, the little witchgirl. Would you kindly send some water to the willow tree, so he can give me some branches to take to the witchbroom maker? He promised to make a fine broom to fly me to the moon."

"Ahhh," moaned the well. "I wished I could. But look and see, a hurricane rolled a stone on top of me. I can't send water to anybody, and I am about to burst! Could you please help me?

"If you would roll the stone off me,
I could send water to the willowtree,
So it could give you branches to
take to the witchbroom maker.
I am sure he could make you a fine broom
so you could fly to the moon."

"Oh, that should be easy!" cried Williwu. And she began to push the stone. She pushed, and she pushed, and she pushed—as hard as she could.

Storyteller invites audience to join her in the pushing motions.

But the stone was far to big to be moved by one little witchgirl. When Williwu realized that all her efforts were in vain [or, for younger audiences, that "she just couldn't do it"], she threw herself on the ground and sobbed,

"Witches spells and witches brew,
I wish I could get rid of you!"

Then she tried all the spells she knew, but nothing worked. Finally she began to cry. Her tears fell all over the stone, which moved him to say, "Little witchgirl, listen to me. You don't need a spell to push me off the well. What you need is a friend."

"A FRIEND?"

"What is a FRIEND?" asked Williwu, bewildered.

"Don't you know what a friend is?" asked the stone, amazed.

"No," replied Williwu, shaking her head sadly.

"A friend is someone who helps you when you need help," explained the stone.

"Listen—go to the white house on top of the hill. It belongs to a little girl whose name is Valerie. She is very nice. Ask her to help you to roll me off the well."

Williwu took a few steps back and said, in a trembling voice, "Is there nobody else who could go in my stead? I've never spoken to any real girls."

"No," said the stone. "As you can see, there is no one else here but you."

And then she heard those words again.

Motion to audience to chant with you.

"It's up to *you* Williwu,
This is something you must do,
If you don't do it very soon,
You'll never make it to the moon.

"All right, I'll try," said Williwu with a sigh. She took a deep breath and ran all the way to Valerie's house.

When she got there she knocked on the door, and Valerie appeared. "I am Williwu," said the little witchgirl, very fast. "Please, will you help me roll the stone off the well, so he can send some water to the willow tree, so it can give me branches to take to the witchbroom maker, who promised to make me a broom so I can fly to the moon."

"Sure," said Valerie "Can I bring my brother Daniel and all our friends along? We were just getting ready for a Halloween party."

"That would be great," said Williwu. "Would they be willing to help us to push the stone away?"

"Of course," said Valerie. "Friends are always willing to help."

Then she called out to her friends inside the house. "Come on, everybody! We're off on an adventure!"

They all rushed out of the house and followed the little witchgirl down the hill. It was a good thing they did come along because it took ALL of them to push the stone off the well.

Storyteller may choose to have help with pushing here.

The well gurgled with relief—and immediately sent huge waterwaves to the willowtree. The willow tree soaked up every drop and gave the children some of its best branches. When they brought them to the witchbroom maker, the kind old man allowed them to stay and watch while he made the finest broom ever . . . long enough so Williwu could invite all the children to come with her to the moon! And the broommaker too!

And off they flew! Now what could be better than a Halloween party on the moon? Williwu, Valerie, Daniel, the witchbroom maker and the children played wonderful new games and danced all kinds of strange new dances until they could dance no more! And never did they meet any of Williwu's cousins because they were partying on the dark side of the moon.

Not before the morningstar rose did they leave. But on the way home Williwu seemed sad, and when Valerie asked her what was troubling her, she began to cry and said, "I wish I wouldn't have to return to my cousins."

"You won't have to return to your cousins," cried Valerie. "Please come with us. We would love to have you."

Nothing nicer could have happened to the little witchgirl. She moved into Valerie's and Daniel's house right away, and it wasn't too long before she became a regular little girl, just like Valerie. And she was never laughed at again or scolded for being good and trying to help.

Optional Ending

The only thing that reminded her of her witchgirl past was one of the dances she had taught her friends on the moon. They loved it and whenever Halloween came around they begged her to sing and to dance that dance with them. In time other people learned it and now you may learn it, too.

Make a circle, repeat the words of the song, and copy the movements of the storyteller.

> See the witches, watch them flying,
> See them rushing through the night.
> Watch the bats come from the belfries
> Come and join their crazy flight.
> Oomba, oomba, sassa, oomba, oomba, sassa,
> yeh, oh yeh, oh yeh, oh yeh.
>
> Watch the wizards from the mountains,
> They are riding on their cats.
> On their heads they carry lanterns,
> In their arms they carry bats.
> Oomba, oomba, sassa, oomba, oomba, sassa,
> yeh, oh yeh, oh yeh, oh yeh.
>
> Come and join their spooky witchdance
> On the night of Halloween.
> They will teach you how to vanish,
> Never more you will be seen.
> Oomba, oomba, sassa, oomba, oomba, sassa,
> yeh, oh yeh, oh yeh, oh yeh.

NOTES

This is one of many original stories that Ruthilde has written. They all strive to help children with making choices. Having grown up in Germany, with its rich folklore tradition, she understands the importance of fairytales and myths as a vehicle for experiencing and interpreting the world, and this understanding informs many of her stories.

IT'S UP TO YOU

It's up to you dear Wil-ly Wu This is something you must do

If you don't do it ve-ry soon You won't make it to the moon

OPTIONAL DANCE SONG

See the witches watch them flying see them rushing through the

night watch the bats come from the belfrys come and join their crazy

flight Oomba oomba sassa Oomba oomba sassa

Yeh oh yeh oh yeh oh yeh

ADAPTED BY
KAYE LINDAUER

The Princess and the Ogre

This story uses visual aids—six posters that need to be prepared ahead of time. See Notes at the end of the story for information about this.

NARRATIVE

AUDIENCE RESPONSE OR TELLER'S ACTION

There was a princess once who had the usual long hair and small feet, but otherwise she was different from most other princesses, and the reason why she was different was this: she didn't want to marry any of the nice young men who kept coming along to ask for her hand. All of them were the sons of kings and therefore perfectly suitable, but still they seemed very dull to the princess, what with their showing off all the time on horseback, and clanking about in heavy armor, and generally making a nuisance of themselves with bad poetry and singing off-key. She wanted instead to marry someone who was very, very clever, and so far no one like that had presented himself.

One day she managed to slip away and was taking a stroll alone in a meadow outside the castle walls when all at once an ogre leapt out from behind a bush and snatched her and carried her off at top speed to his den on a far-off hillside. It all happened so quickly that she didn't have time to pack or leave a message or even call out for help. And before she knew it, there she was, locked up in a little room with the ogre keeping watch on the other side of the door.

"You're mine, dear creature," said the ogre through the keyhole, "and when you've got used to the idea, I'll let you out and we'll have a game of Chess."

If you change your voice to represent the ogre, be consistent—use it each time the ogre speaks, but don't overdo it!

Emphasize the word "chess." Since the ogre says it several times, you can lead the audience to anticipate its coming by emphasis. Exaggerate the OH-H-H! Stamp your foot when you say "Horsefeathers." Since you say this three times in the story, when the audience hears the OH-H cue, they can join in on saying "Horsefeathers." Gesture to let the audience know they can join in!

Now this situation was surprising, to say the least, but the princess wasn't frightened because she knew she could hold her own with any ogre, whether he knew how to play chess or not. She said, through her side of the keyhold, "OH Horsefeathers!"

This wasn't a very ladylike answer, perhaps, but still it was all she could think of to say at the moment. And then she set about looking for some way to escape.

The room in which she was locked was a nice room, considering the fact that it was part of an ogre's den. It looked as if it had been fixed up especially for her. "I fixed it up especially for you!" said the ogre through the keyhole.

There were a table and chair, and a pink-painted bed with a nice pink bedspread on it, and the walls were freshly painted white. That was all, except that on the table were a candle and matches, and a square china dish containing a single needle. And there was one window, big enough to see through but nowhere near big enough to climb out of, even if your feet were as small as the princess's. Still, she peered out and saw that a short way below there was a road running by.

Be very clear about each item, since she is looking for something to help her escape. It is important that you map out the room in your mind: where the bed is located, the windows and the door. This mindset enables you to make appropriate gestures consistently. I myself gesture toward my left when the ogre is speaking through the keyhole, and make a throwing movement with my arm toward my right each time the princess tosses an object out of the window.

"Well, now," said the princess, nodding to herself, "it won't be easy, but much can be done with a needle. I'll get a message ready and when someone comes by on the road, I'll simply fling the message out—a message mixed up in some way that will make it too hard for that ogre to read, but easy for anyone else. Then if the ogre should find it by mistake, he won't know what's going on."

And so, while the ogre hummed little songs to her through the keyhole, the princess set to work. There was no pen to write with and no paper.

How do you think she might make a message with what was in the room? Remember the only tools she has to work with:

> table and chair
>
> pink painted bed, pink bedspread
>
> candle and matches
>
> square china dish
>
> needle.

What can she use to make a message?

Someone may suggest writing a message on the bedspread with a blackened candle wick and tossing the bedspread out the window. *Storyteller:* "Thank you, that is an interesting possibility. Who has another suggestion?" Someone may suggest painting a message on a brick and throwing the brick out the window. *Storyteller:* "Thank you, but remember there isn't a brick or any paint in the room. Nothing is in the room except the objects specifically described."

At this point, the teller is trying to get the audience thinking and involved in the story. If one of the suggestions made is actually part of the story, this information is not revealed right away. The storyteller will have to make a judgment as to how much time to allow for eliciting responses from the audience in order to keep everyone's interest focused on the story. This decision will vary from one

Well, she took off her crown and scratched the following message on it with the needle:

Who knows what this message says? Remember , it is a mixed-up message so that it will be too hard for the ogre to read, but easy for anyone else.

[After code explained:] Then she waited by the window for someone to come along.

After a while, along the road below, a prince on a large white horse came into view. Taking careful aim, the princess flung the crown through the window and down it rolled, bumpety-bump, right to the feet of the horse.

The prince climbed down from his saddle, picked up the crown, and looked at it, and the princess could barely hear what he said:

"Why, here's a golden crown! And someone has scratched it all up with a lot of nonsense, and thrown it away. What a pity—it would have made such a nice present for my little sister if it hadn't been spoiled."

And the prince dropped the crown at the roadside, climbed back onto his horse, and rode away.

But the ogre went down the hill when the princess was gone, picked up the crown, and brought it back to his den, and after a few moments he said through the keyhole, "That's easy, that one. I know exactly what it says." And he read out the answer to the princess. "But it didn't do you any good after all, so you may as well give up and agree to be mine, dear creature, so we can have our game of Chess."

"Well," the princess said, "OH-H-H Horsefeathers!" again.

audience to another, and from one setting to another.

Hold up poster (1) — ASLEEP VASE ENCRISPS FORM GORSE END!

You might wink when you say that the princess used her crown. Of course, they knew she was wearing a crown; she was a princess!

Give the audience time to think. Often someone will decode one word. Ask that person to explain how they broke the code. If a hint is needed, explain how VASE can become SAVE.

Pause long enough before saying ". . . *chess*" to give the audience a chance to say it with you.

Remember to exaggerate the OH-H-H and gesture to the

audience to say with you a strong "Horsefeathers!" (They can see you about to stamp your foot on the word.)

Again, be patient and allow the people to share their ideas, always giving credit for the possibility.

But to herself she added, "Hmm! This ogre is not as stupid as he looks." And she set to work at once on a new message.

This time, she tore a piece of white cloth from the ruffle of her petticoat, and with the needle and a long thread pulled from the hem of her bedspread . . .

"What color was the thread?"

Yes, and with a long pink thread pulled from the hem of the bedspread, she embroidered the following:

What do you suppose this means?

Pause and then ask . . .

You'll quickly receive the answer, "PINK."

Put up for the audience to view poster (2)—decoded, PLEASE RESCUE PRINCESS FROM OGRE'S DEN.

Once the audience has decoded the message, go over it so that everyone understands how it was done: PL plus lots of E's - PLEASE, RES plus the sound of Q - RESCUE, etc.

It is important that the audience stays with you. There is more danger of losing them if you hurry than if you read over the message a second time.

And then she waited by the window for someone else to come up.

Pretty soon a second prince appeared, striding along on foot. The princess took off one of her shoes, stuffed the message into the toe, and flung it out the window. Down it went, bumpety-bump, right to the prince's feet.

"Aha!" he said. "What have we here?" And he picked up the princess's shoe and found the message. "Aha!" he said again. "Here is an odd sort of thing. No doubt it holds answers to some difficult questions of life. But I know all the answers already, so it's not any use to me." And he dropped it by the roadside and went away.

But the ogre went down the hill when the prince was gone, picked up the message and the princess's shoe, and brought them back to his den, and after a few moments he said through the keyhole, "This one is easy, too. I know exactly what it says." And he read it out to the princess.

"But it didn't do you any more good than the first one. So you may as well give up and agree to be mine, dear creature, so we can have our game of—Chess."

Remember to pause to give audience time to say with you the word, "chess."

"OH-H-H HORSEFEATHERS!" said the princess for the third time.

Remember to draw out the OH-H-H and raise your foot to stamp so the audience can anticipate "HORSEFEATHERS" and say it with you.

But she thought to herself, "This is really a rather clever ogre." Nevertheless, she set to work at once on a third message and this time she tried to make it very hard indeed.

Again, ask your audience for suggestions as to what the princess might use to make another message. Encourage them to recall the objects in the room. Repeat each one recalled by a member of the audience.

Expect to hear about the candle and the china dish.

What objects have not been used so far in the story for messages?

She lit the candle, and using the square china dish for a mold, she made a sort of tablet with dripping wax; and when it was cold, she lifted it out and with the needle she wrote the following message:

Put into view poster (3). Read the sign the way it is or ask someone in the audience to read the sign as it is. *Do not yet* work with the audience to decode it.

And then she waited by the window for someone else to pass.

After a while a third prince came rolling along in a golden coach and at the right moment, the princess flung out the wax tablet and down it went, bumpety-bump, and bounded right in through the window of the coach.

Continue to hold up the poster while talking so the audience can study it.

"What's this?!" exclaimed the prince, looking at the tablet very carefully. "Why it's an old shopping list. Anyone who would shop for things like these is no one I want to know!"

And he tossed the tablet out through the window of his coach, signalled to his coachman, and rolled away.

But the ogre went down the hill when the coach was gone, picked up the tablet, and brought it back to his den. After a few moments, he said through the keyhole, "This one is the easiest of all!" And once more, he read out the answer to the princess.

Who has the message decoded?

Make sure everyone understands that the message is clear if you look at every other letter, or if you look at only the capital letters.

Then the ogre said, "You can see that it did you no more good than the other two. Please give up all these messages, won't you, dear creature, and agree to be mine so we can have our game of—Chess?"

Remember to pause before "chess" so audience can join in.

The princess stood on her side of the door, thinking. "This ogre," she said to herself, "is really extremely clever. It is something to be cleverer than three princes put together! We'll see if he is even cleverer than I!"

So she said through the keyhole, "Well, we'll have our game of Chess, anyway, and then we'll see."

So the ogre let her out and in a pleasant room by a roaring fire, they had their game of Chess.

Note: Leave out the "roaring fire" when telling this story in the summertime or in a hot climate.

It went first one way and then the other, and after three hours it was over and had ended in a tie.

"We were made for each other, dear creature," said the ogre, fondly. "Anyone can see that."

The princess said to herself, "This ogre is exactly as clever as I am, myself, no more and no less. Of course, he's rather ugly but, OH -H-H . . . horsefeathers!"

Remember previous instructions when saying, "OH-H-H Horsefeathers!"

Then she said, "Well, looks aren't everything."
And so . . .

Hold up poster (4). Wait for audience to unscramble it. (She decided to wed the ogre!) Then hold up poster (5). Wait for audience to decode. Those who did not quickly decode before may now feel proud to call out an answer. Ask audience after each decoded message to repeat it together. Then hold up poster (6). Again, ask audience to repeat after decoding.

Note: Each of the last three posters (4, 5, 6) say the same thing—which the audience picks up faster as they realize the three posters arrive at the princess's decision.

This group-speaking ends the story experience on a strong note.

SHE DECIDED TO WED THE OGRE!

NOTES

"The Princess and the Ogre" was written by Natalie Babbitt for the 1966 conference of the Children's Book Council, Inc. It was issued to conference participants in pamphlet form as "A Puzzling Story" for *Book Week*, but has never appeared in book or any other form since its pamphlet appearance.

Storyteller's note: Like all of Mrs. Babbitt's literary tales, "The Princess and the Ogre" is written in a superb style, each word carefully chosen. For this reason, I suggest memorizing the story. The contrast of a rather tightly told story with a free spirit achieved through audience partcipation is quite pleasing.

There are six posters that need to be prepared as follows for the story.
• White poster paper is suggested with the lettering done with black magic markers.
• A regular tip as well as a wide tip marker is useful; the wide tip for large letters containing code.
• Posters will last longer if they can be laminated or covered with clear contact paper for protection.

Audience sees:

Reverse side
for storyteller

1. ASLEEP VASE ENCRISPS FORM GORSE END!

1. PLEASE SAVE PRINCESS FROM OGRE'S DEN

Audience sees:

2.

PL+ ᴱᴱᴱᴱ RES+ Ⓠ

🐱PRR + INCE + Ⓢ F+🍶RUM

Ⓞ+🐱GRR'S 🌷🌷🌷-GAR

2. PLEASE RESCUE
PRINCESS FROM
OGRE'S DEN

3.

тHrEe Lʙ. PiG -
мEАтY PoRtIoNs
CHEeSeS
YoGUrT
DOgFoOd
GaRdEn SoD
ʙEaNs

3. HELP GET
PRINCESS OUT
OF OGRE'S DEN

4.

Hᴇ DicᴅEeᴅ Oт
Dᴇw Hᴇт Goʀᴇ.

4. SHE DECIDED
TO WED THE
OGRE

5.

😶SHH +E D+😮HO HUM!+😀🌷━━━

2 🛏-B+W THE

Ⓞ+🐱GRR.

5. SHE DECIDED
TO WED THE
OGRE

6.

аS тHe EnD
sEe CHiLd rEаᴅ
iт, fOr Wᴇ EnᴅiT.
wHᴇE! ʟoNG oRᴅEr!

6. SHE DECIDED
TO WED THE
OGRE

Important: Always give the audience time to think after presenting a poster. Often someone will decode one word. Ask that person to explain how he/she broke the code. A hint may be needed. If so, in poster (1), explain that VASE can easily become SAVE by unscrambling the letters. Ask the audience to repeat it each time a message is decoded. This group-speaking ends the story experience on a strong note. Be sure to tell in advance that this is a story for audience participation.

Riddle Story: In Summer, I Die

NARRATIVE

One morning, we woke up bored. We went to wake someone up. Who do you think we woke up?

So we went to our sister and said, "Sister, sister, wake up— we're bored!"

Can you do that with me?

Sister said, "I'm bored, too." So we all went to find someone else. Who do you suppose we went to next?

So we went to our father and said, "Father, father, wake up—we're bored!"
Father said, "It's too early. Go back to sleep."
So we went to someone else . . .

This time, we went to our grandmother.
We said, "Grandma, grandma, wake up, we're bored!"
But grandmother said, "I would love to do something fun with you. But I need you to bring me something first. Bring me this:

> In summer I die,
> In winter I grow;
> My roots above,
> My head below.

AUDIENCE RESPONSE OR TELLER'S ACTION

Audience: "Our sister."

Say it rhythmically, using rhythmic motions of the hands to mime rocking a sleeping person.
Audience joins in and repeats, "Sister, sister, etc." two more times.

Audience: "Our father."
Say it three times; audience joins in.

Repeat the process of asking who, miming the wake-up, and giving an answer. The children and pets we wake up are all also bored; the adults are all too sleepy.
Continue until someone suggests grandmother.
If no one does, just say:

Say this rhythmically. If desired, add rhythmic hand motions.
Example: first two lines, pat hands on knees. Third line, clap over head. Fourth line, clap with hands close to ground.

We said, "Wha-a-t?" Can you say that like you're puzzled?

> In summer I die?
>
> In winter I grow?
>
> My roots above?
>
> My head below?

Grandmother said, "Well, you'll have to figure out what it is, and bring it to me." So we went off, looking for it, whatever it was. Where do you think we looked first?

So we went downstairs.

What do you think we saw?

The refrigerator! Good idea. Maybe that was what grandma needed!
Let's see; does it die in the summer?
Does it grow in the winter?
Does it have something like roots on its top?
Does it have its head on the bottom?
Good try, but that wasn't what grandma wanted.

We got so discouraged that we said the rhyme as though we felt disgusted:

> In summer I die,
>
> In winter I grow;
>
> My roots above,
>
> My head below.

We may as well go out and play in the snow. So we got dressed in our heavy coat, opened the door, and went out.

Audience joins in the rhythmic saying of the rhyme, with a puzzled tone:

Audience: "In the kitchen."
Mime walking, with hands on knees; audience joins in.
Audience: "The refrigerator."

Audience: "No!"
Audience: "No!"
Audience: "No!"
Audience: "No!"
Repeat asking for guesses (What do you think we saw?) until someone suggests something outdoors. If no one does, say:
Audience joins in, with disgusted tone.

Mime dressing, putting on boots, etc. Audience joins in.
Accept every guess, and try it against the four lines of the riddle, as with the refrigerator. If the audience is not getting the idea of how to guess, call on one of the older ones or even an adult. On the other hand, if someone gives

the correct answer
before you're ready to
let the story end, don't
try that one. Just
acknowledge it as a
good idea, and repeat,

"So what do you think
we looked at next?"
Call on someone else. If
another person guesses,
you'd better accept it,
as below. Use the story
to give progressive
hints: bring up snow
and ice, then mention
icicles in a description.
Finally, bring the
icicles to the fore.

We started to play in the snow. It was good packing-snow,
so we made snowballs; then rolled up great big snow balls,
put one on top of the other, and made a snow-person. It
gave us an idea! Do you think we could be looking for a
snow-person? Does it die in the summer?

Yes, it melts! Does it grow in the winter?

Yes, that's when it's cold enough for snow. Does it have
its roots on the top?

No. Does it have its head on the bottom?

No. It's not a snow-person we're looking for. We were so
disappointed, we started to cry:

> In summer I die (sob, sob),
>
> In winter I grow (sob, sob);
>
> My roots above (sob, sob),
>
> My head below (sob, sob, sob, sob).

We said, "We're lonely. Let's go get our friend, to come
out and play with us." We looked way off: there was our
friend's house. There was smoke coming out of the
chimney, so we knew our friend was home. The roof was
covered with snow, there were icicles hanging down, and
the sidewalk was covered with snow, too.

We ran to our friend's house.

When we got there, we rang the doorbell. How did it
sound?

But no one came out. We knocked on the door. Pretend
you're knocking on the door.

Still, no one came out. We knocked with both hands,
louder and louder, but no one came out!

Audience: "Yes!"

Audience: "Yes!"

Audience: "No!"

Audience: "No!"

Audience joins in, with
sad tone.

Mime running, hands on
knees; audience joins in.

Audience: "Buzzzz."

Audience joins in.

Mime knocking.
Audience joins in.

We knocked so loud that we could hear our own echo. We knocked so loud that the snow started falling off the roof. We knocked so loud that an icicle fell off, and landed next to us. That stupid icicle almost hit us! Wait a minute! Do you think . . .? Does the icicle die in the summer?

Audience: "Yes, it melts."

Does it grow in the winter?

Audience: "Yes!"

Does it have its roots on the top?

Audience: "Yes; no."

Well, the part that attaches to the building is like a root. Is that on the top?

Audience: "Yes!"

Is its head on the bottom? Sort of?

Audience: "Yes!"

We were so excited, we said it excitedly:

Audience joins in, with excited tone.

> In summer I die,
>
> In winter I grow;
>
> My roots above,
>
> My head below.

We each grabbed some icicles and ran home. When we got to grandmother, we were so out of breath that we could hardly say it:

Audience joins in, as though out of breath.

> In summer I die (gasp, gasp, gasp),
>
> In winter I grow (gasp, gasp, gasp);
>
> My roots above (gasp, gasp, gasp),
>
> My head below (gasp, gasp, gasp).

"Is this it, grandmother?" And grandmother said, "Yes, that is just what I wanted. I needed some icicles to chop up. Now, would you like to help me use them to freeze some homemade ice cream?"

And that's just what we did, for the whole afternoon. Then we ate the ice cream. And I can tell you, we were not bored!

NOTES

This story began when I heard a librarian tell the story of a boy being sent to find a "little red house with no windows or doors, a chimney on top, and a star inside." The boy finally finds a red apple with a stem—but where's the star? At that point, the teller produced an apple and a knife, cut the apple in half across the seed pods, and voilá, the seed pods formed the shape of a star.

True Riddles

Folklorists call this kind of riddle a "true riddle." True riddles are metaphorical descriptions of something (e.g., an icicle) in terms appropriate to something else (e.g., a plant with roots). These are different from our common "riddles," such as, "Why did the chicken cross the road . . . ", which folklorists call "conundrums." To get the answer to a conundrum, you have to be told or to read the riddler's mind. But to solve a true riddle, you have only to understand the words and the nature of what is being described. For example, if you know what an icicle is and how it behaves in different seasons, you can solve the true riddle in the story.

At certain ages children seem fascinated with this kind of comparison. As toddlers, their words had only personal, idiosyncratic meanings for them. Later, they learned the literal, shared meaning of much of the language; and now it's as though they are ready to explore the nonliteral meanings again. In this way, true riddles help develop one of the foundation stones of the literary imagination, the ability to think in metaphor.

True Riddles in Stories

The story framework, in its turn, helps children with the true riddle in three ways. First, it lets the teller help children systematically test their guesses, one quality at a time: "Does it die in the summer...?" Second, it removes the onus of making an incorrect guess; we are all disappointed if a guess doesn't work, and the story just continues. When someone guesses correctly, moreover, we all share in the triumph. Third, it allows the teller to give clues as part of the story. This takes away the embarrassment of having to ask for "hints," while keeping up the interest and suspense.

Many true riddles are in prose, just like our common conundrums. But some are rhymed, and well suited to rhythmic speech. This adds a new mode of participation, because metric speech, being more predictable, is easier to join in. So I chose a rhymed true riddle on which to base the story. I added to this the further element of repeating a rhyme or song with a tone of voice that reflects the characters' feelings at that part of the story.

Recast the story to suit your own purposes. I took the opportunity to bring up the frustration I felt as child when I had to wait for adults to wake up on a Saturday morning—and to provide an image of a spunky elder who can do something for young children other than hold them in her lap and rock. As a former teacher, I welcomed the chance the story gives children to bring up possible unorthodox family groupings; and I was also glad to allow practice in dramatic expression of feelings. But you may have other issues you want to touch on.

Once you learn this story, you have learned a framework for many stories. If grandmother (or someone else) sends us off with a different riddle, we have a different story. For example, I make a Halloween story around this riddle, whose solution is "pumpkin:"

>Round as an apple,
>Yellow as gold;
>More things inside it
>Than you're years old.

By way of hints, I take us to a neighbor's front porch decorated with a jack-o-lantern. At the end, we make pumpkin pie. The issue of fear gets lightly touched on, just in the natural course of things.

Related Books

Here are some sources of more true riddles and, therefore, of more stories. Many nursery rhyme books have sections devoted to riddles. Some commonly available ones that I recommend include:

THE PUFFIN BOOK OF NURSERY RHYMES, by Iona and Peter Opie. Baltimore. Penguin. 1963. Paper. The best value in English nursery rhymes. .

THE OXFORD NURSERY RHYME BOOK, by Iona and Peter Opie. London. Oxford University Press. 1955. Hardcover. More complete than the above. .

THE ANNOTATED MOTHER GOOSE, by William S. & Ceil Baring-Gould. New York. Bramhall House. 1962. Another solid collection.

• These collections contain only true riddles (beware: most books of "riddles" contain only conundrums):

BLACK WITHIN AND RED WITHOUT: A BOOK OF RIDDLES, by Lillian Morrison. New York. Thomas Y. Crowell. 1953. Most of these riddles are rhymed. Long out-of-print, but available in many libraries.

WAY DOWN YONDER ON TROUBLESOME CREEK: APPALACHIAN RIDDLES & RUSTIES, by James Still. New York. G.P. Putnam's Sons. 1974. Riddles—some rhymed, some not—and verbal puzzles, all from one section of Kentucky.

CHAPBOOK RIDDLES, by Peter Stockham. New York. Dover. 1974. Small, very inexpensive collection of nineteenth-century rhymed riddles. More archaic-sounding riddles than in the collections above.

• These collections both contain many true riddles from other countries as well as from the United States, Canada and Britain. Since the riddles from other languages are given in translation, they are seldom in verse:

RIDDLE ME, RIDDLE ME, REE, by Maria Leach. New York. Viking. 1970. Grouped by subject.

RIDDLES OF MANY LANDS, by Sula Benet and Carl Withers. New York. Abelard-Schuman. 1956. Long out-of-print, but available in many libraries. Grouped by country of origin.

• If you are interested in the history and cultural evolution of riddles, as well as in riddles from literary sources (as opposed to folk riddles), then read this book:

RIDDLES: ANCIENT AND MODERN, by Mark Bryant. New York. Peter Bedrick Books. 1984.

• The following is the ultimate reference book on English-language true riddles. It's expensive, but invaluable. Organized by the object compared to, with extensive notes and references to other versions, it also contains an index by "solution". So, if you want a riddle whose solution is an egg, you'll find dozens listed, not to mention additional entries under "egg, broken," "egg, hatched," and more. Great for seasonal or holiday riddles; just browse through the index until you find an object associated with the season or holiday. For example, a riddle about a candle might do for Christmas, Hanukah or Kwanza; one about a heart or a letter, for Valentine's Day.

ENGLISH RIDDLES FROM ORAL TRADITION, by Archer Taylor. New York. Octagon Books. 1977 Reprint of 1951 edition.

NORMA J. LIVO

How Raccoons Got Their Masks

INTRODUCTION

One of the most successful works of children's literature is the classic *Millons of Cats* by Wanda Gag. The simple story of an old couple's loneliness and how they chose their special cat from "hundreds of cats, thousands of cats, millions and billions and trillions of cats," has been a favorite for over fifty years.

The refrain is contagious. The use of exaggeration through the words for huge numbers is powerful for young listeners and readers. I wanted to do the same thing for measurement.

I chose a lovable animal for the main character, used the traditional story "threes," royal families, youngest daughter teased by her two beautiful older sisters, and her loyal, modest traits, as themes and motifs. I couldn't resist also employing a "how/why" feature. In trying this story out with children, it works.

It is important for the audience to be familiar with the concept of measurement. Talk about different ways to measure things. Use the king's foot length as a form of standard measure. Measure a few things using the thumb from tip to joint as the inch measure and from the tip of the nose to the end of an extended arm as the yard measure. Compare several individual's measures. Are they the same or different? Why?

Introduce the chain link form of measurement. A chain, surveyor's or Gunter's chain, equals 66 feet. This is because 66 chain links measure 66 feet. (An engineer's chain uses 100 links to equal 100 feet.) Remind the listeners about football officials measuring distances with a chain measure.

Teach the refrain to the audience: "inches of smiles, feet of smiles, yards and chains and miles of smiles." Use hand motions to show inches, feet, yards, chains and miles such as a fish story motion. (How big was that fish?)

Instruct the listeners that everytime the phrase "inches of smiles, feet of smiles, yards and chains and miles of smiles" is used they should join in saying it and making the appropriate hand motions. The refrain is used nine times in the story.

NARRATIVE	AUDIENCE RESPONSE OR TELLER'S ACTION

Once upon a time, in a time and place beyond measure, when the world was brand spanking new and before all raccoons had masks, there lived three raccoon princesses. The two oldest sisters had lovely normal brownish-grey raccoon faces with just the trace of a darker mask around their eyes.

The youngest little raccoon princess had bright sparkling eyes and a cute black nose. She was much plainer looking than her sisters. Her sisters always teased her and called her, "Little No-Mask."

Little No-Mask had something they didn't have though. When she smiled *she smiled inches of smiles, feet of smiles, yards and chains and miles of smiles.*

Repeat refrain and use hand motions to indicate measurements.

She was a sweet raccoon princess. When she caught crayfish she gave them to the royal cook. She loved to hunt for crayfish in a stream with her head up and her outstretched palms moving up and down alternately in the water as she turned over rocks.

When she saw how happy the cook was with the crayfish she brought, she smiled inches of smiles, feet of smiles, yards and chains and miles of smiles.

Refrain

She helped gather shiny buttons, bright pebbles and other gleaming objects she found for the royal treasury. When her father the king admired her finds, she smiled inches of smiles, feet of smiles, yards and chains and miles of smiles.

Refrain

Whenever her parents heard her sisters calling her "Little No-Mask," they scolded the girls and comforted Little No-Mask with the fact that she had more rings on her bushy tail than either of her sisters. When she looked at her tail, she smiled inches of smiles, feet of smiles, yards and chains and miles of smiles.

Refrain

She was always the first raccoon to hear approaching dogs. She would chatter a shrill warning to the other raccoons to get to safety. She would then quickly scamper up the nearest tree herself.

When she saw that all of the other raccoons were safe from the dogs, she smiled inches of smiles, feet of smiles, yards and chains and miles of smiles.

Refrain

Everyone on garbage dump raids loved her. She always found grand morsels of food, which she shared with the others.

Her older sisters spent their time by the pond's edge cleaning and rubbing their light masks with soft moss to keep them beautifully soft and glossy.

One day Little No-Mask discovered a log cabin in the woods. She scampered around looking for a way in. Finally she found an unlatched window and quickly opened it and climbed in. There were lots of interesting things in there.

First, she found a bag of flour. She put her head in and got her face and the tips of her ears all white.

Then she found a can that had the words BLACK PAINT printed on it. She managed to get the top off of it. It didn't smell good but she couldn't resist putting in her paws to see if there were any crayfish there. They came out covered with black, sticky liquid.

She clenched her fists and rubbed her eyes with her paws leaving big black circles around her eyes. She looked like a princess at a masked ball.

Then she saw three sparkling copper pennies on a table and she smiled inches of smiles, feet of smiles, yards and chains and miles of smiles.   Refrain

Now there was something she could take back to the royal treasure chest. She held them in one paw as she gallumped back to the royal tree. She was going into the tree by the big hole near the ground when she saw her sisters.

"Look what I found," she called as she held out her black paw to show them the pennies.

"Who are you?" they asked. "You sound like Little No-Mask but you don't look like her. Who are you?"

She smiled inches of smiles, feet of smiles, yards and   Refrain
chains and miles of smiles at them. They knew it really was Little No-Mask.

"Well, we can't call you Little No-Mask anymore. You have a shiny black mask that is prettier than ours."

She humped her way down to the pond to look in the   Refrain
water and they were right. She smiled inches of smiles, feet of smiles, yards and chains and miles of smiles.

"We will have to call you Black Mask now," everyone told her.

From that day on, the three raccoon princesses played together all the time. Even though all three had masks, you could recognize Black Mask by her inches of smiles,   Refrain
feet of smiles, yards and chains and miles of smiles.

From that day on, most raccoons have a mask and they like to smile a lot.

NOTES

Some background information on raccoons might be apropos. "Raccoon" is an American Indian (Algonguin) name for a small, tree-climbing mammal. They are mainly nocturnal, or active at night, and are extremely curious animals.

"How Raccoons Got Their Masks" lends itself to several extending the story activities.
• Have the listeners see how many other names for "raccoon" they can find. These names could be written in a folder with identifying information about the sources of these names.
• After they become aware of the Native American names, have them search on a map for Native American place names. They could use a dictionary to check name origins.
• Share similar stories. Since "How Raccoons Got Their Masks" explains "how," a natural connection would be to read/hear Kipling's *Just So Stories*.. Have the listeners make comparisons and discuss similarities.
• How many other stories/books can they find that are related to measurements?

Related Books

AISE-CE-BON, A RACCOON, by Lillian Brady. Illustrated by Jerome Connolly. Harvey House. No Date. Using the Chippewa Indian name for raccoon, Aise-ce-bon, the author tells the story of one year in the life of a raccoon.

THE BABY ANIMAL BOOK, by Daphne Davis. Illustrated by Craig M. Pineo. Golden Press. 1973. This is an early-to-read shape book.

BENJAMIN AND TULIP, by Rosemary Wells. The Dial Press. 1973. Benjamin raccoon suffers repeated indignities at the paws of Tulip. He gets his revenge.

BUT NOT STANLEIGH, by Barbara Steiner. Stanleigh Publications, Littleton, Colorado. 1980. Is a photographic essay of life with a family's pet raccoon.

HOW MUCH IS A MILLION?, by David Schwartz. Illustrated by Steven Kellogg. Lothrop, Lee and Shepard. 1985. The illustrations show what a million of some things look like.

LITTLE RACCOON AND THE OUTSIDE WORLD, by Lilian Moore. Pictures by Gioia Glammenghi. Scholastic Books. 1965. Little Raccoon and two little skunks are looking for the outside world and the outside world is full of surprises.

MACROON, by Julia Cunningham. Illustrated by Evaline Ness. Dell. 1962. A raccoon decides to adopt a disagreeable child for the winter months. Then, he really has a problem.

MILLIONS OF CATS, by Wanda Gag. Coward McCann Inc. 1928. A little old man and woman decide to get a cat to be company for them. The refrain, "hundreds of cats, thousands of cats, millions and billions and trillions of cats" is irresistible.

RACCOONS ARE THE BRIGHTEST PEOPLE, by Sterling North. E.P. Dutton. 1966. A factual look at raccoons with 87 remarkable photographs.

RACCOONS AND RIPE CORN, by Jim Arnosky. Lothrop, Lee and Shepard. 1987. The author/illustrator has given us a beautiful wildlife watching experience.

RASCAL, by Sterling North. Dutton. 1963. This is an authentic memoir about a boy and his pet raccoon.

SAVE THAT RACCOON!, by Gloria D. Miklowitz. Pictures by St. Tamara. Harcourt, Brace and Jovanovich. 1978. This is a story about a forest fire and the destruction of the natural habitat. After escaping, raccoon finds a new home.

WHO SANK THE BOAT?, by Pamela Allen. Coward McCann. 1983. One warm day a cow, donkey, sheep, pig and a tiny mouse go for a boat ride. The question is repeated, "Who sank the boat?"

The Little Blue Alarm Clock

Introduction

This story works best with children under ten, although I have also told it to older children and to mixed audiences of children and adults with equal success if the conditions are right. Before beginning, I explain that there is no way, with my one voice, that I can tell this story alone.

"Will you help me tell the story?" I usually ask. "Will you become the sound of [number of] alarm clocks?" (Here you would give the approximate number of persons in the audience. Audience invariably assents.) I continue: "And there's another place, toward the end of the story, when we're supposed to sound like SIX THOUSAND alarm clocks. Do you think you can do it?" (Usually there is a resounding promise of cooperation.)

I then explain how the sounds can be made, more or less in this manner: "Well now, of course, alarm clocks come in different sizes, with different bells and alarm sounds, right? So you can be any type of alarm clock you wish. You can say, 'R RRing..RRRing,' or 'ting ting' or 'R R R R T' or 'BzzBzzBzz' or even 'tinkle, tinkle' [tiny voice]. Or you can do it the way I do it. Here's how I do it: Can you remember how it felt the last time you were very, very cold? 'BRR R R R R R'—your lips stuck together? Sometimes it takes a few tries before I get it. Want to try it with me? Vibrate your lips as you thrust them out . . . BrBBB B BB.

"Now that can be soft or loud. In fact, any of the alarm clocks can sound ANY WAY YOU WANT THEM TO SOUND. You are your own alarm clock, right? Let's try it. Remember, you're going to pretend to be [audience number] alarm clocks. Get ready: One, two, three—ring!" (Audience responds.)

"Marvelous! And now, try to sound like SIX THOUSAND ALARM CLOCKS. Ready? One, two, three—ring! Excellent! Now we can tell our story."

NARRATIVE	AUDIENCE RESPONSE OR TELLER'S ACTION
Imagine a little blue alarm clock who hadn't ever woken anybody up. There he sat on the store shelf, fresh from the factory, waiting to be bought so he could RING his alarm. He was very curious to know how it would feel. In fact he could hardly wait for the chance. In fact, he simply couldn't think of ANYTHING but ringing his	

alarm. It got so his head was full to bursting with it, and he asked everybody around what it was like to ring. But they couldn't tell him. They too, were brand new.

In the end, a gentleman bought him, brought him home, wound him up, and that evening set his alarm for six o'clock precisely. Then the gentleman dropped off to sleep. As you might guess, the alarm clock did not get any sleep that night. He was so excited he counted the minutes away, imagining how marvelous it was going to be when his alarm went off.

"I'll have to be right on time," he said to himself. He was pleased as punch to be behaving responsibly, just like a grown alarm clock.

It was five o'clock already. Five-fifteen. Five-thirty. Five to six—only a few minutes more. "Here we go," said the alarm clock at last. He cleared his bell and he sounded his alarm.

Storyteller makes his/her alarm sound, stays with it ten or fifteen seconds, then exclaims . . .

"OH, THAT FELT WONDERFUL!" To him it sounded like [audience number] alarm clocks. Can you let me hear, now, how it sounded to HIM?

Storyteller makes motion with hands inviting audience to ring their alarms (they will).

Yes, that's how it sounded and it also sounded like foghorns at sea, nine larks, and a rain of silver dollars on a tin roof. ALL PUT TOGETHER. Really, it was MARVELOUS!

This is said over the audience response—not so loudly as clearly.

Hold up hand for silence or bring index finger to mouth in "SHHH" motion.

But what do you think of this? While he was ringing away there, doing his job, loving every second, all of a sudden, he got a conk on the head! Like sixteen mousetraps snapping shut!

When beginning the word "conk," storyteller raises right arm, hand clenched into fist, and brings fist down hard into cupped left hand.

Now that upset him. THAT was no fun! How else could he feel? A conk on the head is a conk on the head, after all.

All day long he kept thinking about it, turning things over in his mind.

Oh, he knew there was a small button on the top of his head. He knew what it was there for, too. It was there so his owner could signal him when it was time for him to stop ringing. But all it needed was a gentle push downwards.   He would have stopped ringing instantly.

[Pause]

Was he conked so hard, maybe, because he was not precisely on time—could that be it?

[Pause]

He felt rather nervous all that night, but in the morning he set off his alarm, precisely at six o'clock. NOBODY could have been more on time. But what do you think of this? He got a CONK on the head, like a rocking chair had smashed over him!

He saw stars. When his vision cleared, he began to think again. Remember how I told you he was a curious alarm clock? Remember how curious he was to know what it felt like to ring, to really ring his alarm? Well, he felt just as curious now to know why he was being smashed on the head, instead of having the signal button simply PUSHED GENTLY the way it was supposed to be.

"Maybe," he thought, "I shouldn't be too much on time. Perhaps the gentleman wants to sleep longer and there's nothing wrong with that. He has every right to. I know! I'll wake him up a quarter of an hour later!"

The following morning he rang his alarm at a quarter PAST six. But what do you think of this! He got a conk on the head bigger than a thunderclap!

That really shook him up! Finally, he got back on balance. "Huh," he said to himself. "If I wake him on time, I get a conk on the head. If I wake him up later, I get conked. I just don't understand people. Could this man be an early bird? All right, I'll try waking him up a little earlier."

When uttering the word "push," storyteller cups right hand in air and gently, slowly moves four fingers close together towards thumb, as though thumb were the alarm button, being depressed by four fingers.

When beginning the word "conk," storyteller raises right arm, hand clenched into fist, brings fist down hard into cupped left palm.

Same instructions as above for word "push."

When beginning the word "conk,"storyteller raises right arm, hand clenched into fist, brings fist down into cupped left palm with greater force than the previous time.

The following morning he set off the alarm at a quarter TO six. But what do you think of this? HE GOT A CONK ON THE HEAD AS BIG AS THE STATUE OF LIBERTY.

Same directions as above for word "conk."

By now, the alarm clock was absolutely desperate. He felt like crying. He was afraid to ring at all. He was so desperate that he couldn't help but come to a desperate decision. He would NOT RING at all.

And indeed, the following morning, there wasn't a peep from him. He just kept silent and waited. Nothing happened. All was quiet. The alarm clock felt as if a weight had been taken from his shoulders. Nothing happened at 6:30. Nothing happened at 7 o'clock.

At last, he thought, at last I've solved the problem.

Nothing happened at 7:30. Nothing happened at 8 o'clock. He rubbed his minute and hour hands together with glee, feeling pleased with himself. But what do you think of this? At 8:30 all of a sudden, for NO REASON AT ALL, he got a conk on the head LIKE A SHIP BREAKING ICE!

Same directions as above on word "conk."

That gave him such a headache, it lasted three hours. When it finally went away, and he could think clearly again, he said, "This is too much. I can't figure it out. I'd better go out and find someone to talk this over with." So he picked himself up and walked out on tiptoe to see if there was another alarm clock out there somewhere with the same problem.

He was in luck. He hadn't gone far when he met an alarm clock that was the image of himself, same dial, same hands, the only difference being that the other alarm clock was red all over.

"Now, then," asked our blue alarm clock. "How do you get on with this waking up business?"

"Oh," groaned the red alarm clock. "It doesn't bear thinking about. When I'm on time, I get smashed on the head. When I ring LATER, I get smashed on the head. If I ring EARLIER—CONK! And when I don't ring at all, I—get—CLOBBERED! Like a ship breaking ice!"

"Well," said the blue alarm clock, "it seems we're in the same boat. Maybe there are OTHERS with the same problem! Let's call all alarm clocks together for a council meeting."

So they sounded the alarm—summoning all alarm clocks to a meeting in [local park] that night.

Storyteller names a local park for meeting place.

Stars were sparkling in the sky when they met, at half past midnight, SIX THOUSAND ALARM CLOCKS SHOWED

UP. All shapes, all sizes, all colors. There they stood, dial to dial, SIX THOUSAND of them, waiting to see what was going to happen. You could hear the ticking, if you weren't sound asleep that night, all the way to [name of adjacent city].

You want to know how it sounded? Well, if you help me, we can do it. Remember these are all DIFFERENT alarm clocks. Some went tick-tock, tick-tock. Others went cluck-cluck.

How else could the ticking have sounded?

Storyteller names adjacent city.

Storyteller curls tongue over top palate for cluck-cluck sound.

Storyteller says, "Yes, that's possible" for anything that sounds reasonably like ticking, but does not let the ticking last too long and distract from the flow of the story.

Finally, the blue alarm clock got up in front of all of them, on a tall box, facing the others and he held up his arms for silence. This is what he said: "Alarm clocks, listen. We love to ring our alarms and there's nothing wrong with that—we are alarm clocks, after all. But do we have to put up with having our heads bashed in for no reason at all?"

"No, no," shouted one.

"We're fed up to the cogs with it!" cried another.

"Alarm clocks," continued the blue alarm clock. "We have a fine job to do. There is nothing finer in the world than sounding an alarm. I propose we go to some place where we can ring our bells WITHOUT being clobbered."

"Hear, hear!" said one alarm clock.

"Great idea!" said another.

And one great big alarm clock in a booming voice said, "Let's not waste any more time. Let's get going now!"

They all began to tick again.

Storyteller uses her/his own ticking sound saying "tick-tock" or making sounds with tongue clucks. Motion for the audience to join in. The ticking goes on like a sound track underneath the story now.

They picked up their little feet and their big feet and they began to walk. They walked and walked and walked and walked until they reached the blue sea.

What joy! A ship was right there, in dock, with nobody around. The clocks quickly got aboard and set sail.

Storyteller motions for ticking to become very very soft by waving

They sailed and sailed until they reached an uncharted island in the [Caribbean, Atlantic, or Pacific, etc.—whichever body of water is closest].

On this uncharted island they could see there was just room enough for six thousand alarm clocks!

"Alarm clocks," said the blue alarm clock leader, "here you see our Promised Land. Here we can ring from morning to night, to our heart's content, without waking anybody."

The alarm clocks were very excited. They shouted, "HOORAY," and scrambled ashore. Then—then—they started to ring, each one ringing just as he liked.

How did they sound? Well, the little blue alarm clock went like? this: "B R R R."

How did the others go?

How did SIX THOUSAND sound?

Oh, really LOUDER than that. Remember these were very happy alarm clocks.

And so suddenly, in the middle of the blue sea, there was this little island filled with the silvery sounds of ringing. It was wonderful. WONDERFUL! How can I describe it? It was like—like there were bells in every wave, in every drop of water. It was like there were nine flocks of larks flying overhead, and sailboats moving along with balloons for sails, all colors.

Each one had [favorite musical group] on board. Can you SEE it all? Can't you just HEAR it all?

---

arms downward from elbow length, palms facing floor, fingers together; or, if preferable to teller, motions for cessation of ticking.

If telling to small children, the storyteller pauses: "'Uncharted' means a place that does not appear on any map, because nobody has discovered it yet."

Waves for the audience to join in.

Encourages louder sound.

Encourages loudest sounds. Let it decrease in sound gradually but keep it going.

This is all said clearly over the sound of ringing. The storyteller has subdued the volume for the best effect.

Optional: Storyteller can improvise his/her own vision here.

Raise your hand if you have the picture there in your mind, because I have something special to tell you.

Hands go up, usually, since everybody wants to hear something special.

OKAY. This is important. Let's wind down the clocks for a rest. EVERYONE who heard those alarm clocks—everyone who SAW that little blue alarm clock moving along from the beginning of his story—is what I call a STORY PERSON. Now, STORY PEOPLE are special people, so since I KNOW WHERE THAT ISLAND IS—truly I do—here's what I am gonna do. I'm gonna ORGANIZE all the story people I can find—and their families—for a STORYTELLING CRUISE right into and through the [Caribbean, Pacific or Atlantic, etc.]. Maybe not this year or next, but one year we will have enough people—STORY PEOPLE—to fill a ship, and we shall sail, and sail, and absolutely visit the LITTLE BLUE ALARM CLOCK and his SIX THOUSAND FRIENDS.

NOTES

Background Information

This story appeared five years ago in *Cricket*, the magazine for children, as "A Home for Six Thousand Alarm Clocks," by Milos Macourek, translated from the Czech by Marie Burg, with pictures by Slug Signorino. It came from a collection of Macourek's stories published abroad by Oxford University Press as *Curious Tales*.

Extending Activities

"The Little Blue Alarm Clock" can easily act as a springboard for a variety of discussions. For example:
• Mention it as an English translation of a Czechoslovakian story. For children in grades 1-6, you can use *Take a Trip to Czechoslovakia*, by Keith Lye, illustrated, published by Watts in 1986. There is a 1972 publication for ages five through nine by Elvajean Hall, also illustrated, entitled *The Land and People of Czechoslovakia*, published by Harper.
• Extend the story into a grand celebration. "What would be the first thing they did, once settled in?" Have a party! Dance, Czech-style! There exists in many libraries a marvelous set of 26 booklets, each containing authentic costume data, music, and specifics on dance steps for *The National Dances of Europe* (Max Parrish & Co., London). In "The Dances of Czechoslovakia," Mila Lubinova explains that Czechoslovakia combines in its folk dances and traditions the colorful wildness of the East with the more sophisticated gaiety of Western Europe, since it is located at the crossroads, so to speak. Her 40-page illustrated booklet mentions children's games with dance played as long ago as the sixth century by Polish, Russian, and Yugoslav children, represented in some of the Czechoslovakian dances at special occasions today.

• Go into feelings. In this case, would you say, for example, that the prevalent feeling was one of FRUSTRATION? Here are two books for preschool children through second grade: *Feeling Frustrated*, by Penny Anderson, illustrated by Dan Siculan, (Children's Press, 1983), and *Frustrated*, by Sylvia R. Tester (Children's Press, 1980).

• You might go into other stories about clocks. For example, *Johnny the Clockmaker*, by Edward Ardizzone, with his own illustrations (Walck, 1960). Practically everyone thought it was impossible for a little boy to try to build a grandfather clock. With the help of just two friends, Susannah and Joe the Blacksmith, Johnny succeeded in proving them wrong. The following list of fiction books for preschool and up is a start:

THE HOUSE WITH A CLOCK IN ITS WALLS, by John Bellairs. Dell. 1974. For grades 3-up.

GUMDROP BEATS THE CLOCK, written and illustrated by Val Biro. Stevens Inc. 1986.

TIK TOK, by Stephen Cosgrove. Price Stern. 1983. For grades 2-7.

CHANGING TIMES, by Tim Kennemore. Faber & Faber. 1984. For grades 6-up.

TICK-TOCK, by Art Seiden. Putnam Publishing Group. 1982. Illustrated.

CUKOO CLOCK, by Mary Stoiz. Illustrated by Pamela Johnson. Godine. 1986.

• Select in advance a book that contains factual data on clocks to make the storytelling an educational experience in the full sense. Following is a list to begin with:

CLOCK BOOK, by Ben R. Berenberg. Illustrated by Art Seide. Western Publications. 1967. A Golden Book for grades 1-3.

TIME & CLOCKS, by Herta S. Breiter. Raintree. 1978. Illustrated. For grades K-3.

TIME & CLOCKS , by Herta S. Breiter. Raintree. 1983. For grades 2-5.

CLOCKS AND HOW THEY GO, written and illustrated by Gail Gibbons. Crowell Jr. Book. 1979. For grades K-4.

HOW DID WE GET CLOCKS AND CALENDARS?, by Susan Perry. Illustrated by Nancy Indereiden. Creative Ed. 1981. For preschool to grade 4.

CLOCKS, by Bernie Zubrowski. Illustrated by Roy Doty. Morrow Jr. Books. 1987. For grades 3-7.

ANNE PELLOWSKI

Mrs. Mondry and Her Little Dog

This story is ideal for closing a telling session. It works best with adult or mixed adult and child audiences. It is especially successful with senior citizens. I start out very briskly, but in a serious tone. In this way, the contrast with the ridiculousness of the later situations shows up better.

I introduce the story by saying it was a popular folktale-type back in the 1920's and 1930's. I indicate that I pieced my version together from fragments told by Felix Moga and from three versions I located by using a folklore index (see Notes). Sometimes I tell the audience I will need their help later on in telling the story; other times I simply begin telling the story, and the audience still comes in at the appropriate times.

NARRATIVE

AUDIENCE RESPONSE OR TELLER'S ACTION

Mrs. Mondry had a little dog. It was a lap dog. She loved that dog so much she took it with her everywhere.

Every week Mrs. Mondry went to town. She had no car so she took the bus. She wanted more than anything to take her dog with her, but she knew it was illegal to take dogs on the bus. One week she decided to do it anyway. She hid the little dog under her coat and went to take a seat way in the back of the bus.

She was so happy! There she was, going to town in the bus, and she had her little dog with her. But hardly had she opened up her coat and settled her little dog in her lap, when there was an awful smell surrounding her. She looked around and there, right behind her, was a man smoking a long, fat cigar. He kept puffing and blowing the smoke right at her. She could hardly breathe.

Mrs. Mondry turned around and said to the man, "Smoking cigars is not allowed in the bus." But he just kept on puffing and blowing smoke at her.

So Mrs. Mondry reached back, took the cigar out of the man's mouth, and threw it out the window!

The man stood up and was about to go and complain to the driver, when suddenly he saw the little dog sitting on Mrs. Mondry's lap.

"Madam," he said, "dogs are not allowed in the bus." And he picked up the little dog and threw it—yes, he threw it out the window!

Pause and look questioningly at audience. Someone will usually supply the answer.

Well, Mrs. Mondry was very upset. She started to cry and just then she noticed they had arrived at the first stop in town so she got out and looked around for someone to help her.

Well, would you believe it, there in the distance she saw—yes, that's right! Her little dog was running toward her and panting like mad.

Pause and someone is sure to say: "Her dog."

But as soon as he came closer, Mrs. Mondry saw *something he had in his mouth!* Can you believe it? There in his mouth was —No! No! Not the cigar! His tongue, of course! Whoever heard of a dog that smokes cigars? No, no, all he had in his mouth was his tongue, no cigar. She was just surprised it was so long, for such a little dog.

Say this very slowly. Invariably, someone will respond: "The cigar." Disregard other responses, point to person who said it, and answer him or her directly.

Well, the next week Mrs. Mondry went to town again, but she decided to walk this time, because she didn't want any trouble on the bus. She put her little dog on a leash, put on her best dress, clasped on her pretty pink pearl necklace and off they went. Well, they had to cross a bridge over a river and Mrs. Mondry stopped to lean over to have a look at how high the water was. Suddenly, as she was leaning over, she heard a plop! like something fell in the river.

She checked and sure enough, what do you suppose had fallen in the river?—

Pause and someone will probably respond: "The necklace." Point to that person and direct your answer to him or her. If someone responds:"The dog," change or add to your narration.

Yes, you got it right this time! It was the necklace. (No, it wasn't the dog that fell in but the necklace.)

Well, Mrs. Mondry was so downhearted about losing her pretty pink pearl necklace that she didn't feel like going to town any more.

"I think I'll go fishing instead," she said.

She changed her clothes, took her fishing pole and bait, and went to the river. She baited the line, dropped it into the river, and waited.

Suddenly, she felt a tug on the line. She pulled hard and the line came in and my goodness what do you think was on the end of it?—No, no, not her pretty pink pearl necklace, and not the cigar either. You got it right, it was a big fish. In fact, it was one of the biggest fish she had ever caught. After that she didn't feel so bad about losing her pretty pink pearl necklace.

She took the fish home, scraped off the scales and then took up her sharpest knife and slit open the fish's belly. Honestly, would you believe it, there inside the fish she found—no, no, not the necklace, just the guts, of course. That's what every fish has inside. No, sorry, she didn't find the necklace, or the cigar, and her little dog was safely by her side. No, all she found was the guts. And she had a fine fish supper that night.

Well, the next week Mrs. Mondry couldn't go to town because her broody hen up and died. It had been sitting on a nice nest of eggs when it just keeled over. Now eggs, in order to hatch out into little chickens, must stay warm, but not too warm. If you put them in a stove, that's too warm. Mrs. Mondry tried to figure out some way of keeping those eggs just the right temperature. Then she hit on an idea. She remembered something she had seen in one of those fancy restaurants in town. She put the eggs in a glass jar and then she set the jar down on a metal holder and under the holder she put a lighted—well, you are clever. You got it exactly right; she put a lighted candle under those eggs in the jar. Well, she watched that candle carefully and never let it go out and when it burned down she replaced it with another. After three weeks she opened that jar and—Oh, my what do you suppose she had?—

No, she had no little chicks, she had a rotten smell! It was awful. (You got it right. She had a big stink. There were no little chicks popping out, just that horrible smell.) Those eggs had turned bad and now they were smelling up the whole house. In fact, the smell got so bad it permeated the air all around her farm.

"I've got to get out of here," said Mrs. Mondry. So she decided to go off to town again, with her little dog. But she had no pretty pink pearl necklace to put on, so she wore her best shoes, even though they hurt when she walked a long time, because the heels were kind of high.

Pause and someone will say "The necklace" or "The cigar." Point to and answer the incorrect ones first; then turn to person saying "a fish," and point while saying "You."

Pause and wait for someone to say "Necklace." If the audience is really with you, they will call out all the previous answers. Adjust your narration accordingly.

Pause. If someone says "Candle," congratulate as if he or she had answered a very difficult question.
Pause. If someone says "Little chicks," answer him or her first. Use other narration to suit other replies called out.

69

Off she went, tottering on those high heels, and soon one of the heels began to get loose and wobbly. All the way to town it got looser and wobblier. Just as she got to town, that heel came off, she tripped and fell, and at first she was disgusted, but when she looked up she gave a smile because she had landed right in front of—yes, that's right, you really are catching on now; she landed right in front of the shoe repair shop. Well, she went in, and there was the shoemaker, repairing someone else's shoes. He was working away in front of that thing—you know—the thing they use to put shoes on to repair them. What is that thing called again? I always forget. It's called a—

You've said it—the last! And that's the last of this story!

(Or: You've said it—the awl! And that's all there is to this story.)

Pause and look at an audience member who has been responding; He or she is sure to say "shoemaker" or something similar.

Pretend to be looking for the right word. Keep pretending to be disgusted that you can't find the word, until audience comes up with one of these two words.

NOTES

While interviewing elderly people in the Pine Creek, Wisconsin and Winona, Minnesota area for background on my historical novels for children, I found a number of persons who were good raconteurs. One was Felix Moga, who told the opening segment in this story (but somewhat differently) and also used the episode of the candle left burning to hatch out the chicks. I was intrigued by these two motifs, and checked them in Ernest Baughman's *Type and Motif-Index of the Folktales of England and North America* (The Hague, Mouton & Co.) 1966; Indiana University Folklore Series, 20. There I found references to similar motifs in tales recorded in the *Hoosier Folklore Bulletin*, vol. 2, 1943. I later found the motifs again in a mimeographed publication of the Wisconsin Folklore Society, edited by Charles Edward Brown (undated, but probably from the 1930's). I put these segments together in my own way. The resulting story is given here, as I tell it.

That Was Good! Or Was It!?

Introduction

I like to tell this story as one last playful bit at the end of a program. Part of the challenge and fun in telling the story is getting the audience to boisterously give their responses. There are many ways to assure this. Below I will give one typical exchange between the audience and me that shows how to "egg them on" to joining in with zest.

ST: I am going to tell you one last story in which you all have a part. You see, all you've got to do is to say all together, "That was good," after I say something that is good; and when I say something that is bad, all together you say, "That was bad." So let's give it a practice run.

ST: The other day I was walking down the street and I found a twenty dollar bill. [Pick something here that has universal appeal to your audience. I might use this for a group of fifth, sixth, or seventh graders.]

AUD: That was good.

ST: No; that was bad because when I got home my mother said I had to turn it in to the police.

AUD: That was bad.

ST: That's the idea, but to make this story really work you've got to be "kooler" than that. It's more like this: "I found a twenty dollar bill." "THAT WAS GOOOOD!" "And I had to return it to the police." "THAT WAS BAAAAD!" Let's try it again.

ST: I didn't get a bit of homework for the first seven periods on the Friday before winter vacation.

AUD: THAT WAS GOOD!

ST: No; that was bad because when I got to period eight the teacher assigned us an eight-page paper.

AUD: THAT WAS BAD!

The response will usually increase 100-fold with just a little "egging."
There are sometimes a few pitfalls for the storyteller to beware of in telling a story such as this.

• For older audiences (5th grade on up) to participate with vigor, I find there needs to be a base of trust between the teller and audience. Somehow the audience must understand that it's all in good fun, and if they join in they won't feel foolish. We all need to feel some element of safety before we participate in any group. Once an audience really likes and trusts you there is very little you can't perform without a proper introduction.

• Often when I tell this story to young people, one or two of them, out of their need for attention, will shout "That was bad" when the correct response is "That was good." Usually all it takes to change this is saying something like, "I know that some of you would like to say 'That was good' when I want 'That was bad,' but this story only works if EVERYBODY gives the correct response and NOBODY messes. Catch my drift?"

• When I first started telling this story, sometimes the audience was a bit confused as to the exact time to chime in with their response. In the beginning, a little conducting of sorts will help them to solve this problem. Then as the audience gets familiar with the timing of the story, all that's needed is to simply freeze in a pose and stare directly at them and they will know when to enter.

• What I'm striving for as the teller is a unified spirited response! I always take the time to make sure the audience is fully participating, even if it means a bit more chiding. There's nothing a touch of humor won't bring out. As tellers we need to read, and work with, our audience.

NARRATIVE	AUDIENCE RESPONSE OR TELLER'S ACTION
Once not long ago, right here in Boston [use whatever town you're in], there were two best friends.	THAT WAS GOOD!
	On occasions I'll find myself changing the response to the "Italian style," i.e., "Thatsa gooda," "Thatsa bada." Or perhaps "Really radical man." "Really bad man." Be playful. Know the audience.
No; that was bad because it was a beautiful Saturday and they had nothing to do. Boring!	THAT WAS BAD!
No; that was good because one of them had a marvelous idea! He had a friend who had a blue- and red-stripped airplane they could borrow . . .	THAT WAS GOOD!
No; that was bad, a real bummer. I mean they had no way to get to the airport . . .	THAT WAS BAD!
No; that was good because they were able to borrow two shiny new ten-speed bicycles . . .	THAT WAS GOOD!
No; that was bad because on the way to the airport both bicycles got flat tires and they'd forgotten the repair kit . . .	THAT WAS BAD!
Well, you see, it wasn't so bad because they were close enough to the airport that they could jog in through the back gate. And so the two friends hopped into the airplane and they were flying high above Boston . . .	THAT WAS GOOD!

Well, not so fast. See, the magnificant motor on the airplane (you know the one I'm talking about?), well, it stopped working. . .

THAT WAS BAD!

Don't worry, it wasn't too bad. See, they had two lovely, nice, neat, incredible (!) parachutes . . .

THAT WAS (!) GOOD!

No; that was bad because when they went to pull the rip cords, the parachutes didn't seem so incredible. In fact, the nasty things didn't open . . .

THAT WAS BAD!!!

Don't worry, don't worry; that was good because when they looked down they could see that directly below them was a huge, soft, inviting pile of hay . . .

THAT WAS GOOD!!!!

Not so fast, not so fast; that was terrible because when they got even closer they could see that there were two sharp, pointed pitchforks sticking up out of that soft pile of hay . . .

THAT WAS BAD!!!!!

Okay, I'll admit things, well, things were looking very bad. But good news—hey missed the pitchforks . . .

THAT WAS GOOD!!!!!!

No; that was bad 'cause they missed the hay stack!!!!

THAT WAS BAD!!!!!!!

And that's the end of this show.

THAT WAS GOOD!!!!!!!!

You better say "good!!!!"

NOTES

I first heard this story back in high school, probably. As a storyteller, I heard it when Pineus James Bancroft-Goslink pulled it out of his bag of tricks and told it as a skit at summer camp. The only written source that I know of is in a book by Alvin Schwartz called *Tom Foolery*.

It's a story that very definitely travels in the oral tradition. As a result, you can use it as a "jumping off point" to explore how much of our cultural and personal history is passed on orally.

Not long ago, much of our history was passed by word of mouth. History lived through the stories, songs, games, news, etc., that were passed from generation to generation by the travelers, minstrels, and bards who carried these things from town to town. When things are transmitted orally they are likely to change a little with each telling. The following ideas will help bring this out:

The Telephone Game: Pass around a circle a sentence that is rich in colorful words, by whispering it into the ear of the person to your right. This is a fun way to show how things change when they are passed on orally.

Story or Song Detective: Take a well-known story like "Stone Soup" or "Little Red Riding Hood"; see how different versions vary and how many can be found. How do these differences occur?

Compare Stories, Songs, Jokes, Games, Etc.: Find several different versions of something and see how they vary. How and why do these sorts of variations occur?

Minstrels, Bards and Troubadours: These folks traveled from town to town with history. Imagine what it would have been like to earn your living from your stories and songs. Every doorway, every hardship could lead to material for a new tale or song.

Writing a Ballad: News was often written into ballads by Minstrels and Bards. Create a rhyming ballad that tells the story of a recent piece of school or community history.

In the clubs, teams, schools, community groups, friends, and families that are part of our lives there is a wealth of stories, songs, games, jokes, cures and dances. Tapping these sources can show how we have a personal folklore or history. The following idea will help bring out some of this information:

Make a List of Common Folklore: Find out what common stories the group knows [i.e. "Eeni-Meeni-Mini-Mo," or "Stone Soup"]. Figure out how and where they were first learned.

Tell a Story From Your Life: Use a theme like the funniest, scariest, most embarrassing thing that ever happened to an individual in the group.

Collect Bits of Folklore: Collect stories, songs, jokes, etc., from parents, grandparents, aunts and uncles. Are they still popular? If they are, why have they survived and others have not. Put together a booklet of the pieces of folklore that you find for families and friends.

Family History and Folklore: What stories, songs, games, special meals does a family have for traveling in the car, at holidays, before bed? Are there customary ways of being called to the supper table, sent to bed, woken up in the morning, meals for certain days of the week? How did these traditions get started? What is your family's history: how and why did they come to America, what does your family name mean, what did your grandparents and great grandparents do for a living? Are there any similarities between families?

Community History and Folklore: How did your town get its name? What stories, anecdotes, and "tall tales" are passed on from generation to generation about the town? Where was the first building, store, hospital, theater, fire station, school located? Are there any noteworthy people from your town? Who were the people who started the town?

BARBARA REED

How Anansi Got the Stories

NARRATIVE

AUDIENCE RESPONSE OR TELLER'S ACTION

Narrator: In Africa, in Ghana, where this story is told, it's not just the storyteller who tells the story. The audience helps too. That's one reason I like to tell African stories. I like to have help. You can help by turning into some of the characters, by chanting, by giving ideas—and of course by listening. Now for this story we must go to Ghana, to Africa. How can we get there? Who has an idea?

[Answers may include] "By airplane," "by boat," "by magic carpet," or "by using our imagination."

Accept the first response and repeat it.

That's *just* the way we'll go! Shut your eyes. . . . You are not in . . . [wherever it is you are telling this story]. You are in Africa, in a village, up in the bush country of Ghana, where these stories are still told. . . . Open your eyes. It's very hot. Can you feel the heat? Can you see the tall palm trees overhead, the small houses with roofs of palm leaves and grass, people sitting in front of their houses, children playing? Now the sun is going down, and . . . here comes the storyteller.

African Storyteller: Ah! I am glad to see you. You have come all the way from the United States to hear our stories? That is good. You have come just at the right time. See, the sun is going down, and that is the time we tell our stories. Story time! Story time!

You are the African storyteller, stepping forward to greet the visitors. The storyteller speaks.

Beating on a hand drum, or shaking a rattle.

Narrator: Every one gathers round—not just the children. In Africa stories are for every one. People are coming out of their houses, from their gardens with digging sticks and baskets, from the river with fish traps. The children are crowding around the storyteller, saying "Tell us a story! Tell us a story! Tell us a story about Anansi!"

African Storyteller: A-a-ah! Anansi!

Narrator: And you know what those children said? Right after the storyteller, in just the same way, they said, "A-a-ah! Anansi!" In African storytelling that is called "Call and Response." The storyteller calls something out and the audience says it right after, in just the same way. Can you do that? Let's try it:

A-a-anansi!

Audience: A-a-nansi!

Do this several times, in different ways, with audience repeating. Do the last time in a whisper.

NOTE: Although children usually have good sense about when to stop Call and Response, following a "that's enough" signal with no special coaching, sometimes an audience gets "carried away" and starts repeating every single thing you say. If this arises, whether from misunderstanding, natural exuberance, or as a form of testing and teasing the storyteller, I treat it as a legitimate technical problem to work out together. We set up hand signals for beginning and ending Call and Response. I do this only if it becomes necessary.

African Storyteller: Very good! You are clever! Have you heard of Anansi in your country? Do any of you know of Anansi? What do you know about Anansi?

Usually hands go up. Someone will know he is a spider. Maybe some children know other things about him. Accept everything.

That's right! Anansi is a spider. He is also a trickster. He loves to play tricks on people.

This routine can be repeated at different points during the story. The first time we do it I concentrate on getting the pattern right. Often it's necessary to remind children that in

African Storyteller: Anansi, the spider!
Audience: Anansi, the spider!
African Storyteller: Anansi, the trickster!
Audience: Anansi, the trickster!
African Storyteller: Anansi, the cleverest of all!
Audience: Anansi, the cleverest of all!
Narrator: At least Anansi *thought* he was the cleverest.

African Storyteller: This is the story of a time in Anansi's land when there were no stories. Can you imagine that? No stories. People were sad. They had each other, they had food and work and even music, but no stories. One day Anansi called all the people together.

Anansi: What can we do? It is Nyamé, the Sky God, who has all the stories. It is not fair. We need the stories. They should belong to us. We must get Nyamé to give us the stories. Do you think he knows we want them?

Anansi: Do you think Nyamé could hear us if we called him? Let's try.

Call and Response, the storyteller speaks first, then the audience, *in unison*, like a song, so they don't start racing to be the first to say it. Taking Call and Response seriously as something worth doing just right makes it more enjoyable. In the rhythm of the chant I stroll as Anansi, moving my arms in a spidery way. I encourage children to do the same, move like Anansi, imitate me, or invent their own way.

Repeat several times, ending with the last verse.

This last line, said in a different voice, in a way to discourage Response, is when you find out if children already have a sense of when to stop chanting in Response, or whether you have to be explicit and practise.

Speak to the audience as if they are the people of Anansi's land and you, Anansi, are consulting them.

NOTE: Children will offer perfectly reasonable solutions that would spoil the story. Accept these as good ideas, but find a way around them. For example: "We can make up our own stories." "Yes, we *can!* But these stories Nyamé has are our stories, too, and we should have them."

77

Anansi: Great Nyamé!
Audience: Great Nyamé!

Anansi : Nyamé, the Sky God!
Audience: Nyamé, the Sky God!

Anansi: Give us the stories, *please!*
Audience: Give us the stories, *please!*

Anansi: No answer. I guess Nyamé didn't hear us. Maybe he would answer if we drummed for him. Drum like this, with your hands on your legs.

Anansi: Oh no! It's no use. Everybody sit down and be quiet and let's think.

Anansi: Nyamé is too far away. He doesn't hear us. What can we do? Who has an idea?

Narrator: Anansi's people gave him lots of ideas. He tried first one and then another, but nothing worked. Finally he said:

Anansi: I, Anansi, will climb up to the sky land and speak with Nyamé.

Audience: Get a ladder and go up and ask him.

Narrator: Anansi reached up and pulled down the sky ladder and started to climb it. The wind blew and the ladder started to sway back and forth.

Anansi: I need two people to hold the ladder steady.

Call and Response:

In a rhythmic, chanting voice.

Repeat, then pause and listen.

Show how to drum different rhythms, with cupped hands on thighs, in Call and Response pattern. Add clapping, chanting, dancing. If musical instruments are available, pass out a few. This is worth the time it takes because of the way it gets everyone involved. When you want to end it, sit down conspicuously on the floor and say loudly:

Wait for every one to settle down and collect any musical instruments before going on.

If you start getting suggestions that don't work, like rockets or airplanes keep admiring them but keep asking for more suggestions until you get something semi-usable like "a bird."

One way or another you have to get Anansi up there. Best for the story if he either pulls down a sky ladder, or gets other spiders to help him make a web ladder.

If the first child you call on says this you are home free. *Anansi:* Good idea!

Pantomime the actions as you tell.

Get a couple of people to hold the bottom of the ladder as you

Audience: You could spin a spider web and climb up it.

Anansi: That's a good idea. I could spin a web. But I am just a little spider and Nyamé's sky land is a long way off. I will need all the spiders in the land to help me. Can you all be spiders and help me spin a web ladder to the sky?

Anansi: Spin a web
Audience: Spin a web
Anansi: Weave a ladder
Audience: Weave a ladder.

Anansi: Oh, that's a fine ladder. Thank you, spiders. Now I can climb up and ask Nyamé.

Narrator: Anansi climbed and climbed. He looked down at his people below and called down to them.

Anansi: Don't worry. I will speak to Nyamé. He will give me the stories.

Narrator: Anansi climbed all the way to the top and stepped out onto the clouds. He saw a tall, tall man walking towards him. It was Nyamé, the Sky God.

Nyamé: What are you doing here, Anansi?

Anansi: Oh, great Nyamé, I have come to ask you for the stories. My people, they have no stories. They need them so much. Please, great Nyamé, give us the stories.

Nyamé: All stories belong to Nyamé.

Anansi: Oh, but Nyamé, we would give you great honor. We would say "This story comes from the Great Nyamé, the Sky God.

Nyamé: There is a very high price on the stories. I do not think you could pay it.

Anansi: Please, what is the price?

Nyamé: You must bring me three things: Mboro the hornets, Osebo the leopard, and Onini the python.

climb. Remember to release them later with a "thank you," so they don't go on holding all through the next scene.

Children will follow you, chanting and pantomiming weaving the ladder.
Call and Response. Pantomime pulling a cobweb strand out of your middle.

Pantomime making a rung of the ladder

Repeat, as the ladder gets higher and higher.

Pantomime as you tell, climbing ladder, looking down, waving, climbing some more, stepping off the ladder onto the clouds. Show by contrasting postures and voices which is Anansi and which is Nyamé.

Anansi: Oh yes, thank you Nyamé. I will do that. I will bring you those three things. I will bring you the price. Thank you.

Pantomime of bowing, backing away, climbing down ladder, etc.

Narrator: So Anansi climbd down the ladder and when he was almost down he called to his people.

Anansi: I spoke with Nyamé. He said I could have the stories. Well, he *almost* said I could have them. I just have to bring him a few things.

Narrator: Anansi went to his garden

Pantomime walking to the garden along a path that winds around and through the children. As you walk, repeat

Call and Response.

African Storyteller: Anansi, the spider!
Audience: Anansi, the spider!
African Storyteller: Anansi, the trickster!
Audience: Anansi, the trickster!
African Storyteller: Anansi, the cleverest of all!
Audience: Anansi, the cleverest of all!

Narrator: At least Anansi *thought* he was the cleverest. He picked two gourds—do you know what a gourd is?

If some one knows, let them tell the class. Otherwise describe it briefly, with its hard outside and seeds that rattle inside.
Pantomime picking two gourds and shaking them to hear their rattle.

Anansi: Will you hold these gourds for me? Hold them tight.

Pantomime giving gourds to two children to hold.

Narrator: Anansi took out his knife and cut a hole in each gourd.

Pantomime.

Anansi: That's right. Now shake the seeds out. Thank you.

Narrator: Then Anansi went down to the river and filled one of the gourds with water.

Anansi: Do I hear the buzzing of Mboro the hornets? Do I hear some buzzing?

Audience obliges by buzzing.

Narrator: Anansi started sprinkling water from the gourd all over the hornets

Pantomime.

Anansi: Ah Mboro, you are foolish hornets! Why do you stay out in the rain? Come into this nice dry shelter. You can wait in this dry gourd until the rain is over.

Narrator: The hornets flew into the dry gourd, zzz! zzz! zzz! zzz! and Anansi took a handful of leaves and stopped up the hole. [Pantomime.] When he shook the gourd the hornets were angry and buzzed. [As you shake, the children will buzz.] But when he stopped shaking the hornets were tired and stopped buzzing.

Building this cue into the story—when you stop shaking the gourd the hornets stop buzzing—is a good way to make sure the buzzing stops when you need it to.

Anansi: Ah Mboro, you are *very* foolish hornets, and now I will take you to Nyamé.

Narrator: So Anansi climbed the sky ladder with a gourd full of hornets—there are times when it is useful to have eight arms and legs. He looked for Nyamé.

Pantomime climbing ladder

Anansi: Nyamé, see: I have brought you Mboro the hornets. Would you like to hear them sing? Now may I have the stories?

Approach someone in the audience, thereby turning this person into Nyamé.

Shake gourd. "Bzzzz—" Stop shaking. Buzzing stops. Hand gourd to Nyamé.

[Nyame refuses].

Anansi: Oh that's right. I forgot. I have to bring you two more things. Osebo, the leopard and Onini the python. I will bring them.

Well, it was worth a try. (Aside to audience)

So Anansi went down the ladder without the stories.

Pantomime bowing to Nyamé and starting down ladder.

Anansi: Listen, my people. Nyamé wants me to bring him Osebo, the leopard. How can a little spider like me capture a big dangerous leopard? I need your help. How can we capture Osebo?

Audience: Set a trap.

Anansi: What kind of trap?

Audience: Dig a pit.

Anansi: We need some people to dig a pit. Do you have something to dig with? Get your digging tools. Where shall we dig the pit?

Choose about six people.

Oh, that's good. That is just in the path where Osebo walks every day, down to the river to get a drink of water. I will climb up in this tree and supervise.

Narrator: When the trap was finished, the people left quietly and hid, so Osebo wouldn't hear them. Do we have an Osebo?

Narrator: What kind of a noise do you think Osebo made when she found she was in the pit?

Anansi: Oh Osebo, what are you doing in that pit? Would you like me to let you out? I would like to, but I am afraid of your terrible claws. I'm afraid you will kill me. I have an idea.

Narrator: Anansi took a young tree by the edge of the pit, bent it over and staked it to the ground. He tied a vine to the tree and lowered the other end into the pit.

Anansi: Osebo, can you tie this vine tightly around your front paws, so your terrible claws won't hurt me?

Narrator: As soon as Osebo's paws were tied, Anansi cut the rope that was holding the tree down, the branch sprang up and Osebo was yanked up out of the pit, and there she hung, dangling in the air.

Anansi: Nyamé didn't say whether he wanted Osebo dead or alive. What do you think? Dead or alive?

Audience: Dead! Alive!

Anansi: If Nyamé wants her dead and I take her up alive, he can always kill her. But if he wants her alive and I take her up dead, he might be angry. Help me tie her up.

Narrator: Thank you, tree.

Children really get into the pantomime of digging a pit. As Anansi you can decide with them when the pit is deep enough and get them to cover it with branches and leaves. They may add details like bait, or a net. When it's time, cut off the action and move the story along.

Children return to seats.

Choose an Osebo and accompany her padding along the path with the drum, giving a loud rumble when she falls into the pit.

If Osebo doesn't roar, let the audience roar for her.

Give Osebo a chance to answer, but if she doesn't, just keep going.

Choose someone to be a tree.

Help Osebo and the tree with this pantomime.

There are many other ways of capturing Osebo that children may suggest, spring trap, cage, net, etc. Go along with whatever they come up with and let them work out how to do it. Just as long as Osebo ends up captured, alive and harmless.

Rarely a consensus.

Pantomime.

Child playing tree returns to seat.

Anansi was too small and weak to help dig the pit, but he was not too small and weak to carry Osebo all the way up the sky ladder.

Anansi: See, Nyamé, I have brought you Osebo, the leopard. See her fine coat, her beautiful markings, her fierce teeth. Now may I have the stories? . . . Oh, that's right. There is still another part of the price, Onini the python.

Narrator: Thank you, Osebo.

Narrator: Anansi went down the ladder, thinking about that python. It is no easy thing to capture a big snake like a python. Anansi took a long bamboo pole and walked back and forth, near where he knew Onini lived, saying aloud to himself:

Anansi: My wife says he is shorter, but I say he is longer. My wife says he is shorter. I say she gives him no respect. He is longer.

Narrator: Anansi heard a hissing sound—do I hear a hissing sound? Onini put his head out of the bushes. Will you be Onini?

Anansi: Oh Onini! What a coincidence! You are just the person who can settle our argument. My wife says you are shorter than this pole, but I say you are longer. What do you think? How can we tell?

Perhaps we can measure. If you could lie down beside this pole then we would know for sure whether you were longer.

Anansi: You seem a little short. Can you stretch further? The trouble is, Onini, when you stretch out one end, the other end shrinks up. If you let me tie your head to one end of the pole, then it won't slip when you stretch your tail.

Narrator: So Anansi tied Onini's head to one end of the pole.

Anansi: Now stretch your tail, Onini. Just a little more. Here, I will tie your tail so it will not shrink back and we can prove how long you are.

Narrator: Anansi tied the tail of Onini to the pole, and wound Onini so tight with vines that he couldn't move.

Pantomime carrying Osebo up the ladder, with her paws still over her head. Present her to a different Nyamé.

Every time a child has joined in the action and is no longer needed it is necessary to thank them and release them to sit back down again.

Children will hiss. Better, quicker and less disruptive to choose a child who looks ready, or one you think would benefit from the opportunity, than to issue a general call for volunteers.

Pantomime laying pole on ground. Onini lies down beside it.

Pantomime.

Pantomime.

Anansi: My wife was right. You are shorter than this pole. You are also very, very foolish. Now I can take you up to Nyamé, the Sky God.

Narrator: Thank you, Onini. Anansi picked up Onini the python and carried him up the sky ladder and gave him to Nyamé.

Child playing Onini returns to seat.

Do not involve a child in being Nyamé this time. Do all this next part yourself.

Anansi: Great Nyamé, I have brought you all three parts of the price: Mboro, the hornets, Osebo, the leopard and Onini, the python. Now may I have the stories?

Narrator: Nyamé, great Nyamé the Sky God, looked down at Anansi.

Nyamé: Yes, Anansi, you have paid the price. You have done what nobody else could do. You have earned the stories. They are for you to tell and to share with your people. Here are the stories.

Narrator: And he gave them to Anansi in a covered basket.

Anansi: Oh thank you, thank you, Nyamé, thank you.

Bows and hugs the basket

Narrator: Anansi could hardly wait. He ran as fast as he could to the ladder, clutching the basket of stories. When he was part way down he called to his people,

Anansi: I have the stories! I have the stories!

Narrator: But then Anansi started to think, "These are my stories. They were given to *me.* I worked very hard to get these stories." He had forgotten that Nyamé had given him the stories to share, that every one in the village had helped him. "It is not right that I should have to give these stories to other people. They are mine."

Anansi was thinking so hard about the stories that he lost his footing and started to fall. The cover of the basket flew off and stories started to fly out and blow away. Anansi fell and fell until he landed on the ground, and he quickly scooped up all the stories he could find and put them back into the basket.

Pantomime of falling through the air.

Pantomime. You are down on the floor picking up the stories. Tell this next part, kneeling on the floor, looking up.

But the other stories, they floated all over the world, like milkweed seeds. If you reach up, very gently, and take one, now you have a story too. And that is why, although Anansi the spider has many stories, every one in the whole world has a story to tell.

84

Now we have to leave the country of Ghana, leave Africa and go back to . . .[wherever it is you are telling the story at this moment]. Shut your eyes . . . . now open them, and here you are.

As storytellers in Ghana sometimes say at the end of a story, "That is my story, be it bitter or be it sweet, take some for yourself and leave the rest for me."

Stand up. It's important to bring the children back to where they started.

NOTES

Presenting the story

My approach to participation storytelling is conditioned by my background in creative drama, and strongly influenced by Mara Capy, whose course, in 1975, in "Ethnic Story-telling Through Movement" changed my life and first set me on the storytelling path. One of her specialties is African participatory storytelling, and I find her style the most absorbing and certainly the most risk-taking of any participation storytelling I have encountered. To say I have been strongly influenced is not to say I attempt to emulate her. I am a different person and, as we all do, I start with the inspiration and adapt it to what I can do.

As I look at the various ways the audience is invited to "join in" the story of "How Anansi Got the Stories," I see several types of participation, of varying degrees of risk.

On the **low risk** level are chanting and making sounds all together; low risk for the children because every one around them is doing the same thing, low also for the teller, who has planned it and knows how it will work. A slight risk, perhaps, because an older group might balk at doing it, but the dignity of the name, Call and Response, and the formality of trying to do it just right seem to raise it safely above that dreaded baby level. There's also a risk for the teller—or would be if you didn't anticipate it—in having the sound go on too long once you have activated it. You will see I have dealt with that in the notes that accompany the story.

Medium risk is eliciting suggestions and asking children to play roles in the story. At least three-quarters of a younger class is eager to help act out the story. The eagerness of older children new to storytelling is not immediately apparent, but is there. I work up slowly to having them join the action, asking a couple of people to hold the ladder, or hold the gourds, before we get into anything more active or demanding. The risk level rises when I surprise some child by approaching her with the gourd of hornets and saluting her as Nyamé. However I protect her by treating her very respectfully, and making it work, whether she answers yes or no or says nothing at all. Some risk of surprises here for the teller, but just enough to make it fun—nothing you can't easily handle. Usually, by the time we need to dig the pit, there are more than enough raised hands clamoring for the opportunity. I don't ask for volunteers, just choose people briskly, balancing boys with girls and eager outgoing types with their more timid buddies. Once children are part of the action I like to allow room for their creativity, so I try to avoid telling them exactly what to say or do. Suggestions, since I accept them all, are no particular risk for the children, but can present many interesting hurdles for the storyteller. The risk is losing the story, but once you start saying this is right and this is wrong, children will fall into the all too familiar pattern of guessing what you as teacher want them to say, and much of the fun and all of the spontaneity goes out of it.

At first the awkward suggestions are innocent and well intended. The **high risk** part comes when children realize that they can say *anything* and you will use it in the story. They may start deliberately throwing more and more impossible things at you. The teller has to think fast, but fortunately children do not demand that you think of a *good* solution. Anything will be appreciated. After you show you can handle it good-humoredly, you can end it by becoming Narrator and going on with the story. Usually it stays good-natured and fun, but sometimes it does go over the edge (it's a risk, right?) and children get giddy and raucous. How can you close down the giddiness without putting down the children? In the character of Anansi you can say, "That is enough! That is enough! You give me so many ideas my head is whirling," and then have Anansi do whatever he needs to. Children know that Anansi is willful and slippery, so this can happen within the framework of the story. Or you can be very still, look up at the sky and as Narrator say quietly, "But the sun was going down, it was getting dark, story time was almost over and the story was not ended. Sit quietly now and I will tell you the end of the story." Or, you can get out of character and just tell them that it's now your turn and you are going to finish the story.

Sometimes time is getting short and you have to turn off the participation no matter how smoothly it is going. To save time I often narrate rather than act out the capturing of Onini the Python. Whatever calming device you use, the thing that makes it work is that the children truly do want to hear how the story ends. Many get distressed if they think things are getting out of hand. They've had fun helping with the story, but now they want to hear how it ends and they settle right down. As in the well-known folktale, before one says the magic word that starts the flow of salt, pasta, porridge or creativity, it is good to know the magic word that stops it. Fortunately you have both words firmly in your possession, because you are the Storyteller.

Why take these chances and risk letting things get out of control? It puts playfulness and spontaneity back into storytelling. It gives children a chance to put *their* ideas into the story, even when they aren't *your* ideas. Children see that you respect their ideas. At the same time they see your commitment to the story. You may allow the story to be changed somewhat, but not destroyed. It becomes a game, with the children challenging you and you meeting the challenge.

The story also works fine without getting into the high risk area. You have to assess what you are comfortable with and what the class you are working with can handle. With some classes I tell this story quite straight, with just a little gentle participation. With some classes I wouldn't do this story or any participation story. Since I go into a classroom as a visiting artist, I also alert and consult the classroom teacher when I am considering doing something which might get the children excited and noisy. I may tell the class that I wouldn't do this with every class, but I think they can handle it and ask them if they'd like to try. Afterwards I thank them, and since they were my partners I give them a chance to say how they think it went. I point out to the teacher the good things I noticed. If some children are left with ideas they didn't get a chance to express, I may suggest writing or making a picture story of their idea for the story.

I also know there are people who may find all this very mild and who are confident and successful in opening things up a lot wider than I dare to. I salute you, and would like to visit one of your classes.

Sources of the Stories

I have adapted this traditional tale from several sources. I first encountered it as "All Stories Are Anansi's" in *The Hat-Shaking Dance and Other Ashanti Tales From Ghana*, by Harold Courlander and Albert Kofi Prempeh (Harcourt Brace, 1957). The ending is adapted from another story in the same book, "How Anansi Got All the Wisdom." I have also read the story in Courlander's *Treasury of African Folklore* (Crown, 1975), and in Gail Haley's *A Story, A Story* (Atheneum, 1970).

The cultural background comes from reading about Ghana and Ghanaian storytelling and from listening to and talking with Ghanaian storytellers and musicians, and others who have spent considerable time in Ghana and other West African countries. My introduction to the rich possibilities of African participatory storytelling came from my first storytelling teacher, Mara Capy. My sense of speech rhythms and patterns has been affected by working with a percussionist who does Ghanaian drumming and has accompanied me in a program of "African Drum Tales."

Finally, it is the many children I have told the story to and with who have shaped my particular telling of this particular tale.

Related Books

As with any good story, this story can lead children in a number of different directions. Such as:

1. More Anansi Stories

Anansi is endlessly appealing, whether getting away with his clever tricks or overreaching with his greediness and getting caught and embarassed. After an introduction to this West African spider trickster hero, children are usually eager to hear other Anansi stories. All of these books include some cultural background.

THE ADVENTURES OF SPIDER, WEST AFRICAN FOLKTALES, by Joyce Cooper Arkhurst. Little. 1964. A good collection of short stories, that lend themselves to telling by children.

ANANSI, THE SPIDER, by Gerald McDermott. A picture book with brilliant abstract African designs. Anansi's six sons, who have wonderful names like See Trouble and Stone Thrower are very satisfactory to act out in a patterned rhythmic way.

ANANSI, THE SPIDER, by Gerald McDermott. 16mm film. Landmark Educational Media. 1969. The animation and the music add to the impact of the book. Experiencing the film and the book, hearing the story told and acting it out would give children a rich multi-sensory multi-arts experience.

THE HAT-SHAKING DANCE AND OTHER ASHANTI TALES FROM GHANA, by Harold Courlander and Albert Prempeh. Harcourt Brace. 1957. These twenty-one humorous Anansi stories lend themselves to participation and elaboration, and are also enjoyable told straight, or even read aloud.

A STORY, A STORY!, by Gail Haley. Atheneum. 1970. A Caldecott winning picture book of Anansi's quest for the stories.

ANANSI, THE SPIDER MAN, JAMAICAN FOLK TALES, by Philip Sherlock. Crowell. 1954. Anansi gets around, travelling to the Islands with African slaves, and is just as tricky and successful dealing with Caribbean flora and fauna.

THE DANCING GRANNY, by Ashley Bryan. Atheneum. 1977. Now in the Antilles, Ananse, the ever greedy, lures Granny with his irresistible music into dancing away and leaving her garden unprotected.

2. More African Stories for Participation

If it is the "joining in," that particularly appeals to the children, stories from other parts of Africa, not just from Ghana and not just about Anansi, also lend themselves to participation, because so much of African storytelling is participatory.

THE VINGANANEE AND THE TREE TOAD, by Vera Aardema. Warne. 1983. Spider in this Liberian tale seems to be a hard-working fellow, unlike Anansi. It is tiny tree toad who defeats the terrible Vingananee monster. The repeated sounds (ideophones) invite children to join in the sounds with accompanying actions. ("Fras, fras, fras," as each animal in turn sweeps with the broom.)

WHY MOSQUITOES BUZZ IN PEOPLE'S EARS, by Vera Aardema. Dial. 1975. Leo and Diane Dillon won a Caldecott medal for their illustrations for this cumulative West African tale.

WHY THE SUN AND THE MOON LIVE IN THE SKY, by Elphinstone Dayrell. Houghton Mifflin. 1968. A legend of Southeastern Nigeria, illustrated by Blair Lent. Children like walking in procession, following the drum beat, being the water and water animals filling Sun's house so full that there's no room for him and his wife Moon and they have to rise to the sky.

WHY THE SUN AND THE MOON LIVE IN THE SKY, by Elphinstone Dayrell. 16 mm film, based on the book. ACI Films. 1971. Telling the story first is a necessary introduction to enjoying this film because of the difficulty in understanding the narration at first hearing.

3. More About Spiders

If it is spiders that capture children's interest, Anansi stories could lead a class into a study of spiders, going back and forth from fact to fiction, and at the same time helping overcome the fear of spiders that some children—and adults—carry around with them.

SOMEONE SAW A SPIDER, by Shirley Climo. Crowell. 1985. A nice collection of spider facts and stories, including Native American ones like "The Spider Brothers Make a Rainbow."

A FIRST LOOK AT SPIDERS, by Millicent Selsam. Walker. 1983. Selsam's *First Look at . . .* science books are written clearly and simply enough for young readers, but are informative for any one of any age needing a first look.

THE WEB IN THE GRASS, by Berniece Freschet. Scribner. 1972. Roger Duvoisin illustrates the miracle of the spider web.

CHARLOTTE'S WEB, by E. B. White. Harper. 1952. The contrast, between the personalities of wise kind Charlotte in this beloved book, and rascally Anansi might give children permission to create a spider character of their own to tell a story about, including some spider facts.

ADAPTED BY
GEORGE SHANNON

Lazy Peter

NARRATIVE

Peter lived with his grandmother on the top of a mountain where autumn came early and spring came late. Even though the mountain was not that big, Peter had never been down to the bottom since he'd learned to walk. He'd never walked to the bottom because he figured out if he went to the bottom, he'd have to turn around and walk back up for supper. And why go to all that work to end up where you started from? Truth was, Peter never did a thing but eat and sleep. Whenever his grandmother asked him to do this or that, the only thing he ever did say was, "Wellllllll, I'm tired. I think I'll take a nap."

He was so lazy he hadn't changed his clothes in five or six years. They were dirty, to be sure. But even more, he had kept growing and the clothes had not. His sleeves and pants were way too short and nothing would snap or button. Peter didn't care, though. He never went out of the house. All he ever did was sleep or eat or say, "Wellllllll, I'm tired. I think I'll take a nap."

One morning his grandmother finally gave up. She ate her breakfast, went to work in the garden, came straight home that night, made herself supper and went straight to bed.

"Grandmother," called Peter. "I'm hungry. You forgot to make my supper."

But all his grandmother said was, "Wellllllll, I'm tired. I think I'll take a nap."

Peter was so lazy or dumb he never thought to get his own food. He sat at the table all night long. He was still there waiting for his supper when his grandmother got up and made herself breakfast the next morning.

He was still there that night, waiting for yesterday's supper, when she came home again, ate supper and went

AUDIENCE RESPONSE OR TELLER'S ACTION

Pause

Pause

Pause. Invariably, audience will join in at this point.

89

straight to bed.

"Grandmother, I'm hungry!" called Peter. "I want some food."

She said, "Welllllll, I'm tired. I think I'll take a nap."

Pause. Audience will join in.

"Grandmaaa!" he yelled, "my stomach is growling and grumbling and hurts. I want some food RIGHT NOW!"

"Welllllll, " she said again. "I'm tired, but I suppose I have enough strength to do one more thing."

She got up, grabbed her broom, and swatted and swept him right out of the house. And as he was rolling down the mountain, she called out, "And don't come back till you're ready to work. I've had enough!"

Peter rolled and tumbled down the mountain and when he finally stopped at the bottom, he just said, "Welllllll, I'm tired. I think I'll take a nap."

Pause for audience to join in.

The next morning as he was trying to decide if he wanted to roll over, get up or take another nap, a little old man walked by and said, "Yes, indeed. I've got just the thing for a boy who looks as hungry as you. You give me your coat and I'll give you this harmonica. First time this harmonica makes music, it will get you lunch. Second time this harmonica makes music, it will keep you out of jail. And the third time this harmonica makes music . . . well, I'm never too sure, but you'll find out."

Sure or not, Peter wanted lunch. He said, "Yes," and the trade was made.

The man walked off with the coat, and there sat Peter with the harmonica. Now he'd never had a music lesson in his life and didn't know a single song. But he had seen a peddler play once. And he remembered you had to blow and move it back and forth, like eating corn on the cob. And since Peter loved corn, he knew how to do that. He began to play, and even though he didn't know a single song, a song came out.

Teller begins to snap fingers in correct rhythm, invites audience to join in.

As he was playing, a woman came by on her way home from market. She had two big baskets filled with breads and fruits and vegetables. As soon as she heard the music, she began to tap. Her hips began to sway about and soon she was dancing as fast as could be. For the special thing about that harmonica's song was that whoever heard it HAD to dance! They could not stop! That woman was soon dancing all over the place, and as she danced, her baskets spun around and around. Her food was flying everywhere.

She screamed, "STOP!" But Peter kept on playing and playing until all the food had bounced out of her baskets and onto the ground.

When he finally stopped playing, the woman was so tired she had to sit down and rest her feet. And as she rested, Peter began to eat his lunch. All the food that had bounced to the ground.

Teller cues audience to stop music.

The woman yelled, "Stop! That's mine!' But Peter just said, "Finders keepers," and went right on eating.

She kept yelling and he kept eating until two farmers came up and asked, "What's the trouble here?"

"The trouble is that boy," she said. "He's stealing my food."

"If he's stealing," they said, "sounds like we ought to tie him up and take him off to jail."

Well, as soon as Peter heard the word "jail" he knew what he needed to do and he did it fast.

He began to play the harmonica again. And this time the woman and both farmers had to dance. They cried out, "STOP!" But Peter played faster, faster, and faster still. The faster he played, the wilder they danced and the more they got tangled up in their rope. Peter kept on playing until they were so tied up and tangled, they couldn't do a thing but wiggle on the ground with their feet waving in the air. And when they couldn't do a thing but wigggle on the ground, Peter stopped playing.

Teller begins music and audience joins in.

Teller cues audience to stop.

Then he smiled and said, "Do have a nice day."

By then Peter was feeling very good. He'd had lunch, kept himself out of jail, and best of all he had that harmonica. He started back up the mountain to show his grandmother what he'd found.

He called, "Grandmother, look!' as he walked in the door. "I've got this harmonica and it makes people dance and we can have anything we want. What do you want?"

"A smarter grandson," she said. "Harmonicas can't do that. And besides, you couldn't make enough music to make enough money to buy all we need. Now give me that thing."

She grabbed it, meaning to toss it into the fireplace and stop all the nonsense. But as she held it in her hand, she remembered how her grandfather had taught her a few harmonica songs when she was a girl.

Wondering if she could still play one of the songs, she put it to her mouth and began to blow. And a song came out, but none she remembered. It was the song that came out when Peter played! The song that always made people dance!

Teller begins music and audience joins in.

With his grandmother playing, it was lazy Peter who had to dance! He went whirling and spinning all around the room. He yelled, "Please stop!" But his grandmother kept on playing. She liked the song. It was a real toe tapper. And besides, she'd never seen that boy move so fast. He was dancing under the tables and over the chairs. She played for hours before her lips gave out and she had to stop.

Teller cues audience to stop.

When she finally did stop, Peter couldn't do a thing but collapse on the floor and try to catch his breath. And while he was trying to catch his breath, he saw his grandmother go over to her trunk where she kept her treasures. She took a little key off the ribbon around her neck, unlocked the trunk and put the harmonica inside. Then she locked the trunk tight, put the key back on the ribbon around her neck and smiled a big smile.

And from then on, Peter knew that nobody could get that key to open the trunk to get the harmonica and make people dance EXCEPT his grandmother. And knowing that, he began to work around the house. Inside and out. Every day. All day.

And any time he began to get lazy or say, "Wellllllll, I'm tired. I think I'll take a nap," all his grandmother had to do was to walk near her trunk and smile as she held up the key.

And just the thought of having to dance so fast and long sent Peter right back to work. So, since the day it was locked away, no one has heard that harmonica play.

NOTES

Lazy Peter has worked best for me with upper elementary age children and family groups where the humor can be appreciated and motor skills are up to the rhythm of needed participation. Frequently as a way of bonding with the audience I will talk about people being lazy in general and joke with them about the fact that maybe there could be some lazy people among them . . . but none as lazy as the boy in this story. Once the audience and "I" know one another I explain that this story works best if they will help me. "There is a song with this story and everytime the music starts I need you to help make the music. I'll sing and anyone who wants to may sing along, but your most important part is keeping the rhythm going. Can you snap like this? (I demonstrate the snapping rhythm.) Good. If your fingers get tired you can use your hands and knees, but fingers work best with so many here. Sometimes we'll do the music together and other times I'll be telling part of the story while you keep snapping the music. You'll be the soundtrack just like a movie." Though I obviously can't sing and tell at the same time, I continue to snap fingers while telling to help maintain the rhythm AND to encourage the children to keep snapping Then I will sing and snap through the song several times so that everyone feels familiar with it. "Now in this story, the music will start and stop several times, but you'll know when to snap and when to listen by listening to the story. Everybody ready?" (they nod yes, etc.) And I immediately being: "Peter lived . . ."

While I believe Lazy Peter sounds and flows like a folktale it is more like a folktale's second cousin twice removed. Its now distant relative is a Spanish folktale I read in print several years ago called "Lazy Carlos and the Enchanted Fiddle" in the *The Big Book of Stories from Many Lands*, edited by Rhoda Power (Watts, 1969). As I told it time and again I began to consciously give it a more North American setting and tone, and let the story continue to recompose itself via audience reaction to and acceptance of my alterations in the tale's exterior elements. As it is printed in this collection it is a transcription of the tale as I have shared it with upper elementary-age children, and family groups across the country.

Any dance music or rhythm will work well with the story. I suggest that the teller use one that he likes very much and one that will always come quickly to mind. The melody that I use comes from an eastern European folkdance, which I have danced to. The following is a rough transcription of that melody.

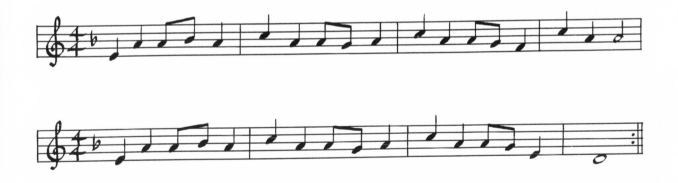

LAURA SIMMS

Sunman

NARRATIVE

I am going to tell you one of the oldest stories in the world. It is based on a Bushman myth from Africa. You can help me tell this story. In many places in the world children and adults join in with song and gesture. Let me teach you the refrain in the story, so you can sing it along with me.

> Sunman, Sunman, Bring us your light
> Sunman, Sunman, Chase away the night.

Now let's add these gestures. Good.

Sing the song two times.

Cross your arms near your waist and then lift them up, stretched out.

Repeat the song and gestures two or more times.

In the earliest times there was no day, and there was no night. The earth was covered by a grey mist.

The people could not see things far away. The people could not see things nearby.

One day a boy was born, a boy who had a great ball of light under his armpits. It was as round as a sweet melon. It was as large as an ostrich egg.

When he lifted his arms it was day, and when he put down his arms it was night.

Put up your arms for "day," and down for "night."

He was called the Sunman.

Everyone loved the Sunman. Because when he awoke, he put up his arms and it was . . .

When he put down his arms it was . . .

Let the children respond "light" and "night."

People could see one another. The children could go out to play. They could see the food they were eating. They could see things far away. Everyone loved the Sunman. And everyone sang the Sunman song.

Song and gestures.

Sometimes the Sunman grew tired. In the middle of the

day he would put down his arms. Everyone would call out...

His arms would go up and there would be light.

Repeat the song two times.

You can repeat this with gestures two times.

Time passed. The Sunman grew old and the Sunman grew tired of keeping his arms up all day long. So one day the Sunman crawled into a cave and went to sleep.

The people went to the mouth of the cave and they sang...

But the Sunman did not wake up.

The people called and they clapped and they sang and they stamped. But the Sunman did not wake up.

The earth grew dark and cold. The people grew sad.

One day the old people called to the children and they said:

Tilt your head as if to sleep.

Repeat song two times.

If you are in a large open space, call the children together in a circle as if you are seated around a fire outdoors. Let them act out the rest of the story with you guiding them. Choose one child to be the Sunman asleep.

"Children go quietly."

"Children go carefully."

"Go to the cave where the Sunman sleeps."

"Lift him in your arms and take him outside and throw him up into the sky."

Have the children repeat.

Have the children repeat.

Have the children repeat.

Have the children repeat, along with gesture of throwing him into the sky.

The Sunman flew higher and higher. He just kept spinning until his arms spread open and there was light. But the Sunman rose higher and higher in the sky. He spun faster and faster until he turned into a ball of fire. He was not a man anymore. He was the sun.

The people still sing his song.

After throwing gesture, keep arms up and watch him spin.

Arms open.

Repeat the song two times, arms up and down.

The Sunman is still in the sky. You can see him. From morning until evening he walks across the sky. At night he sleeps. And everyone still sings his song.

NOTES

I have always been fascinated by the life of the Bushmen who live in the Kalahari Desert in South Africa. I read every book I could find about them, listened to recordings of their beautiful music, and viewed documentaries. I have a great respect for the directness with which they relate to one another and their environment.

Once while working with a group of young children, I retold this story. We were telling stories about how things came to be. As I told the "Sunman," the children, accustomed to participation stories, spontaneously put up their arms and repeated my words. I had them enact the story. That night I made up the song.

I have read two versions of this myth. But for my performance I have extracted the essence of the story and put it into my own words to bring it alive. I removed certain elements of the story that were purely cultural, but maintained the feel of the narrative. Being able to do that comes from having ingested a great deal about the Bushmen and their storytelling, and also from uncovering the basic "universal" meaning in the story.

It may interest you to hear about the Bushman storyteller who told this tale. His name is "Old Kau," and he is described as follows: "Old Kau excelled at telling stories. He was something of an actor, illustrating his tales with mime and gesture. Now and then he jumped up to imitate some animal or other in his narrative and delighted the children with his antics." And from the same source, there is this description of storytelling among the Bushmen: "In the evenings the children sit with adults listening to their conversation. They soon pick up song and dance by imitating their elders." (See below, THE HARMLESS PEOPLE, pp. 144,141)

I once told this story at the Martinique Hotel in New York to a group of thirty children ranging from ages two to twelve. Afterwards, a little girl pointed to the window and said "Sunman," and she and her mother left the room singing the song.

In order to tell the story with heart, it is important to recognize what this story offers the children. Of course it offers a chance to imagine the Bushmen, but more than that, it allows them to imagine themselves interacting with nature and helping their village to have light. (You could talk about what the sun provides, both positively and negatively. You might also discuss why the light may have been under the boy's armpits.) Also essential to the telling of the story is the natural cycle of birth, growth, old age and transformation through death. In a traditional culture, like this African culture, it is always the old people who pass on their wisdom to the young; and the young who are given responsibility to act for the benefit of all.

This is a bold and simple story that in its telling and in its responsive quality is impacted with meaning and image and delight.

Related Books

THE HARMLESS PEOPLE, by Elizabeth Marshal Thomas. Knopf. 1959.

WITH UPLIFTED TONGUE, by Arthur Mankowitz. South Africa. Central News Agency. 1956.

KALAHARI, by Jens Bjerre. New York. Hill and Wang. 1960.

THE HEART OF THE HUNTER, by Laurens Van Der Post. New York. Harcourt, Brace Jovanvich. 1961.

AFRICAN MYTHS AND TALES, edited by Susan Feldmann. Dell Publishing. 1963.

AFRICAN FOLKTALES, by Roger D. Abrahams. New York. Pantheon. 1983.
AFRICAN ART IN MOTION, by Robert Farris Thompson. Univ. of California. 1974.
PRIMAL MYTHS: CREATING THE WORLD, by Barbara C. Sproul. Harper & Row. 1979.
SKYGODS: THE SUN AND MOON IN ART AND MYTH, by Katherine Komaroff. Universe Books. 1974.

SUNMAN

Sun man   sun man   bring us your light

sun man   sun man   chase away the night

Ah ——————

Paper Flower

NARRATIVE

As I tell this story, I will illustrate it by making some things out of paper. Watch carefully; after the story is over, we will all learn how to make these things and lots of new variations besides. But first, the story:

Long ago in old China, a very large family lived on a very small farm. They all worked hard together, but sometimes they could not raise enough food and they were hungry.

One day the oldest child, Peach Blossom, spoke to her parents. "I am old enough to go out into the world and look for work. I could support myself, and you would have one less person to feed here on the farm."

Although they knew Peach Blossom's idea was a good one, her parents were very sad to have her leave. She promised that after one year she would come home for the holidays, to visit and tell the family about her adventures.

Peach Blossom travelled from town to town looking for work, but farm work was all she knew how to do, and city people did not need a farm hand. Finally she found a family that needed help. They had the laziest, the most spoiled children you ever met!

I'm sure you know how to make your own beds. And set the table, and take out trash, and feed the cat, and lots of other things? Well, these children never lifted a finger to help their parents the way you do. So their parents hired Peach Blossom to do all the children's work for them. The work wasn't hard. She didn't even mind the children whining and nagging at her all day long. But they complained, "Peach Blossom is too pretty a name for a servant. She's just a country girl. We'll call her Mud Pig!"

So it was, "Mud Pig, pick up our toys! Mud Pig, wash the dishes!" She waited eagerly for the year to be over so that she could visit home.

But when the holidays came, the people she worked for would not let her go. "We need you now more than ever, Mud Pig!" they complained. "We need you to decorate the house, and cook the special foods for our feast, and help us with our holiday clothes! You can't go now, Mud Pig."

"I promised my family I would come home for the holidays," Mud Pig explained patiently. "Please pay me so that I can go."

Then they got a very clever, mean idea. "You can go, Mud Pig, but only after you finish three jobs for us. You must bring us: fire wrapped in a piece of paper; and water wrapped in a piece of paper; and wind wrapped in a piece of paper."

Mud Pig was amazed. What strange jobs? Can you picture what would happen if you tried to wrap fire in a piece of paper?

Or wrap water in a piece of paper?

> Mime pouring water on a sheet of paper and trying to wrap it up.

Or wind?

> Mime trying to catch a breeze

She realized these tasks were impossible. They were just a trick to prevent her from going home! And then, thinking of home, she remembered how she and her little brothers and sisters used to play with scraps of paper when they had no other toys. She remembered that sometimes they used to fold a square piece of paper in half *very carefully*, like this: they always matched the edges *just right*, and pressed the fold with a fingernail to make it nice and *sharp*.

> Hold up a square of paper
>
> Figure 1 a.
> Press folds against a tabletop or the wall behind you. Hold up the rectangle, folded side down.

Then they would bend a light crease across near the top like this, to show how far to cut; and then they would cut fat 'fringes' from the *bottom* fold *up* to the light crease, like this . . .
then they would open it up . . .
and bend it around like this: . . .
to make a PAPER LANTERN!

> Figure 1 b.
>
> Figure 1 c.
> Figure 1 d.

They would put a bottom in it, and a handle on it, and then they could carry a lighted candle in it—without the flame touching the paper. Fire wrapped in a piece of paper!

> Set down lantern, take second square.

She also remembered how they used to make a paper drinking cup. Turn the square so it looks like a diamond.

Figure 2 a.

Fold the bottom point up to the top, making a triangle:.

Figure 2 b.

Fold it sharp with your fingernail! Then bring one lower point (C) up to the opposite side.

Figure 2 c.

Not too high—not too low—but about in the middle, so that this edge (EC) runs from side to side just like (parallel) the bottom fold. Now bring the other lower point (D) up across (to E) too.

Figure 2 d.

Press them sharp with your fingernail. Now there are two *flaps* in front, and two loose *points* (A&B) on top. Take the front point (B) and tuck it down inside the front flap.

Figure 2 e.

That will keep the flap from flapping. Now open the cup with your fingers—you can see it's a PAPER CUP now—and tuck the back point (B) down inside.

Figure 2 f.

Now Mud Pig could carry water wrapped in a piece of paper!

Figure 3.

There was just one more "impossible" task for Mud Pig to do. She took a third piece of paper, folded it in half like the first one, and began to pleat it back and forth from one end.

Finish pleating the FAN while you continue the narrative.

Mud Pig was ready to go home to her family now. She took her three paper things to the people she worked for. "I have done as you ordered," she said. "Here I bring you fire wrapped in a piece of paper—

Hold up LANTERN.

and water wrapped in a piece of paper—

Hold up CUP.

and wind wrapped in a piece of paper—"

Hold up FAN.

They were surprised and angry. "Wait a minute, Mud Pig! You had to do all three tasks. You have brought the fire and the water, we see them. But where is the wind in that piece of paper? You failed the third task; you must stay."

Mud Pig replied, "There is wind in this piece of paper. You must shake it to make the wind come out."

Wave the fan close to listeners' faces, making their hair blow about visibly.

"You see? I have done all three tasks. Now pay me, so that I can go home."

Set down these paper items, take a fourth sheet, and continue telling the story as you follow steps in Figure 4 to make the PAPER FLOWER without commenting on your actions.

They had to let Mud Pig go.

When she got home, her family was delighted to see her. She told them all about her adventures in the city, and how lazy and mean those children were.

"But it was the only job I could get," she pointed out.

When the holidays were over, she got ready to return to the city. "I've been thinking," she said. "It seems that the city people do not know how to make useful things out of paper. Perhaps they would like to buy paper lanterns, and cups, and fans. I could start a business!"

Mud Pig went back to the city, but she did not return to work for those lazy, mean children. Instead she made paper things and sold them; first from a basket on the street, then from a wagon, and then she bought a shop. She sold so many paper things that she sent for a sister and brother to help her. Soon their business was so good that people asked, "Why does such a successful woman have such an ugly name as 'Mud Pig'?"

It is a Chinese custom to change your name to make it fit you. So she changed her name to—PAPER FLOWER.

Roll up fringed strip very tightly; fluff out fringes.

Hold up your completed FLOWER.

NOTES

This story/activity works well with children in school or library settings and is excellent for intergenerational groups such as family parties. It is totally nonreligious (the Chinese 'holiday' is unspecified), but it introduces paperforms which can be developed into colorful decorations for Christmas/Hanukkah gift packages, mobiles, garlands, tree-trimming, etc.: see Variations under MATERIALS, below.

The activity, however, should follow listening to the story/demonstration. When everybody tries to learn, fold, and cut during the telling, plot is forgotten by the time everyone's ready to go on to the next incident. Save the creative chaos for the end. Telling takes eight to ten minutes. Participants' learning, practice and improvisation can continue for up to an hour!

Students as young as kindergarten can make satisfying paperforms, but hasty folders may be disappointed with sloppy, unrecognizable results. Even little fingers readily learn to *match edges precisely* and *press all folds sharply* to produce satisfying, good-looking items. It's worthwhile to belabor these points while telling the story and while teaching the forms.

Do demonstration folds against a wall, tabletop, or on an overhead projector. Maybe you can work in mid-air, but kids who imitate you risk disappointment. The distinctions between 'fold' and 'crease', 'point' and 'flap', etc., were developed to avoid confusing learners. Whatever terms you use, use them consistently. Some listeners will already know how to make one or more of the forms. Deputize them as valuable assistant instructors.

MATERIALS NEEDED:

When telling the story and teaching the folds, use very large scissors and big paper squares (newsprint or computer printout). It is not necessary to finish the Lantern or to fasten the Fan or Flower while telling: just hold them in position for show and go on. Provide learners with scissors and practice squares cut from scrap such as discarded dittos or waste computer paper. Newspaper advertising circulars have bright colors which don't rub off on hands like news-ink.

Variations: For holiday decorations, embellish plain paper with crayons, markers, glue and glitter, etc. Use fancy giftwrap, foils, tissues. Encourage experiments with different widths and depths of fringing or pleating; different angles of folding; pinching the fan in the middle instead of at one end. Use thread loops or pipecleaners for hanging ornaments.

LANTERN lends itself to a wide variety of strip widths. It looks very fancy lined with a different color: glue layers together before beginning.

CUP can hold candy or tiny presents. Or, it becomes a BELL when pressed open and hung upside down. Make tiny bells for earrings, all sizes for mobiles.

FAN can be fastened and hung in many different ways (bow? wings?). Vary the pleat width for a variety of effects.

PAPER FLOWER becomes a fluffy pompon when made from tissue paper: white snowballs, colored blossoms.

Each group produces variations I have never seen before. The real challenge is to control a happy accident in order to repeat it.

Background Information

"Paper Flower" is an original story built upon an oriental motif: solving "impossible" tasks through papercraft. A number of Chinese and Korean stories tell of an imperious mother-in-law who demands fire or wind wrapped in paper from her witless daughters-in-law; a clever country girl provides them with the Lantern and Fan. I used a different plot for "Paper Flower" and added the paper Cup and Pompon. The traditional stories, taken from turn-of-the-century collections of Chinese folk and fairy tales, have been reprinted and retold as:

"Precious Jade," in *The Skull in the Snow,* by Toni McCarty (New York: Delacourt Press, 1981).

"The Young Head of the Family," in *Tatterhood and Other Tales* , by Ethel J. Phelps (Old Westbury, NY: Feminist Press, 1978).

"The Girl Who Used Her Wits," in *My Book House* (vol 4), edited by Olive Beaupre Miller (Chicago: The Book House for Children, 1937).

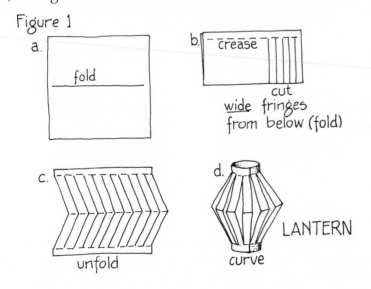

Figure 1

a. fold

b. crease cut
wide fringes
from below (fold)

c. unfold

d. LANTERN
curve

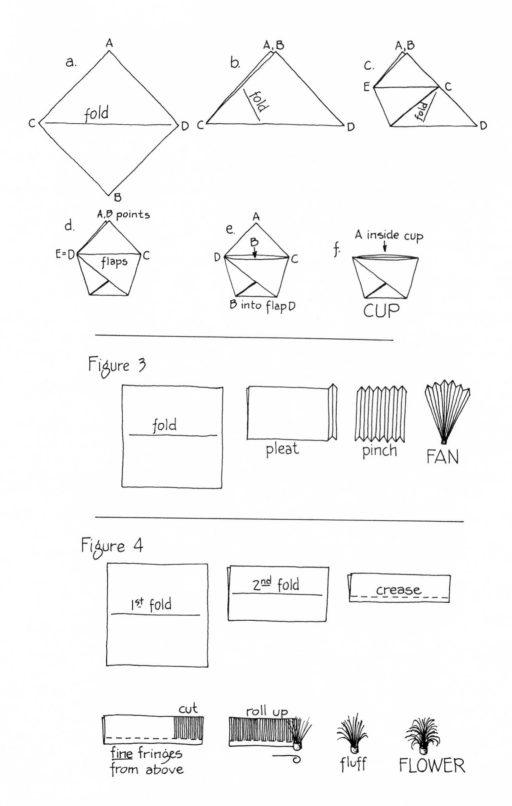

a. A fold C D B

b. A,B fold C D

c. A,B E C fold D

d. A,B points E=D flaps C

e. A B D C B into flap D

f. A inside cup CUP

Figure 3

fold   pleat   pinch   FAN

Figure 4

1st fold   2nd fold   crease

cut
fine fringes from above   roll up   fluff   FLOWER

RUTH STOTTER

Aga-boog-a-way X-nay-snaze-nay

NARRATIVE

In San Francisco there lived a boy named Steve who loved to go fishing. One day Steve decided to fish from the old army pier beneath the Golden Gate Bridge.* He took a sandwich for his lunch. Do you know what kind of sandwich he took?

Steve also took some bay shrimp* in a jar. He thought he might catch a salmon, or a . . .

It was a beautiful day, and Steve threw out his line and sat on the pier waiting for a fish to nibble. He waited a long time. Finally, the little plastic red and white ball tied to his fishing line began to bob up and down. That meant he had a bite! Slowly, very slowly, Steve reeled in his line.

AUDIENCE RESPONSE OR TELLER'S ACTION

*Substitute the local, and regionally known fishing places and types of bait to arouse more interest.

Look at audience inquisitively. When someone suggests a kind of sandwich, nod your head and say, "Yes, that is what he took, a [kind of] sandwich." You are establishing the precedence of the audience filling in the blanks.

Pause and wait for audience suggestions.

Repeat everything that is called out so that everyone hears what is mentioned. This also gives participants positive reinforcement.

If a fresh water fish is suggested, you can say, " You must know Steve! he caught a[kind of fish in well-known lake nearby] the week before!"

Stop and mime this action in such a way as to invite listeners to join you.

As he pulled in his line, Steve looked to see what he had caught. But there wasn't a fish at the end of his line. Oh no, instead there was . . .

Wait for audience suggestions. Select one and repeat the sentence.

After carefully removing the [kind of fish] from his line, Steve decided to throw it back into the ocean.

Steve put another shrimp on his hook and cast his line again. He sat on the pier to wait. He waited and waited.

Pause and mime a few attitudes to suggest waiting (e.g., hands behind head, yawn).

Optional story stretch here.

Anyone else have an idea what he did while waiting?

Point to audience members, who create different poses indicating Steve waiting for a bite.

Just when he was ready to give up and go home, Steve felt a pull. The red and white bobbin was going up and down! Something was on the end of his line! Once again, slowly and carefully, Steve reeled in the line.

Mime, inviting participation.

He could see something hanging from the hook. But it wasn't a fish. Oh no, instead there was a . . .

Wait for audience suggestions. Select one, being sure to repeat clearly each and every other suggestion made first.

Yes, it was a [kind of fish]. Now, Steve didn't want a [kind of fish]! Quickly, he threw it back in the ocean.

"I'll try one more time," he decided. For the third time he cast his line.

Mime, inviting participation.

He watched the red and white bobbin bounce on the waves. Then, suddenly—it disappeared! It was under the water; that meant he had a bite! Once again, slowly and carefully, Steve began to reel in his line.

Mime, inviting participation.

And there was his catch—a cap! A faded blue denim cap with a visor that was curiously unfaded. "Oh well," thought Steve. "I'm tired of fishing anyhow. I might as well take my catch home. Maybe I'll wear it to cool off my head. That sun is pretty strong." He wrung out as much of the water from the cap as he could and clapped it on his head. It hadn't sat there for a minute when a strange feeling came over him.

"AGA-BOOG-A-WAY X-NAY-SNAZE-NAY!" he shouted right out loud. And immediately felt foolish. Where in the world—what in the world—why in the world—. Before he could figure out what happened, he felt an odd, tingly feeling shoot right through him—like he wanted to *do* something, something mischievous, something bold, something he'd never done before.

As he walked home with that cap on his head, he passed a corner where fresh cement had just been poured. There was the usual string of posts around the edges to keep people from stepping on the new piece of sidewalk. He looked around to make sure no one was around, picked up a stick and began to scratch in the cement. Do you know what he wrote?

Repeat each suggestion offered, responding with "No, not that," "Good idea, but that is not what he wrote," etc., and then choose the most outrageous.

THAT'S IT! That's exactly what he wrote, with illustration, while chuckling, "Great, just great. I've always wanted to draw and write in wet cement."

Just then a man wearing a construction hat came from behind the building. "What are you doing there, kid?" he yelled. "I'll get you for that!"

Steve ran. Jumping over a fence, he found himself behind the grocery store. He hid behind the recycling bins until he didn't hear anything and thought it was safe to come out. As he crept around the bin, he saw the bottles inside. "Hmm, it sure would be fun to smash some bottles," Steve thought. He picked up a . . .

This can be used as an opportunity for more suggestions from the audience, or you can make your own choice of bottle.

[kind of bottle] and threw it on the asphalt parking lot. Pieces of glass flew around as Steve hurled brown and green and clear glass bottles onto the asphalt. A grocery clerk came running out of the store. "Hey, stop that!" he yelled. Steve turned and ran, circling in front of the market. There was fresh fruit displayed in front of the store, and as he ran by, Steve reached out and grabbed a . . . What do you suppose he grabbed?

Repeat audience suggestions, and then select one.

YES! That's exactly what he had in his hand when Mr. Sutter, the grocery store owner, saw him. "Why, that looks like that nice little boy, Steve. I'm really surprised to see him do a thing like that. I'll have to call his parents."

When Steve got home, he pulled off his cap and left it on the table in the front hall, went up to his room, and put on his stereo and his earphones to listen for awhile. Not long afterward, Steve's sister, Susan, came home. She saw the cap and got an irresistible impulse to put it on. Which she did. Immediately, she screamed, "AGA-BOOG-A-WAY X-NAY-SNAZE-NAY!"" And suddenly she felt odd, tingly, like she wanted to *do* something, something mischevious, something bold, something she'd never done before. "What should I do?" she wondered. "I know! I've always wanted to paint a mural on the living room wall."

She ran to get her coloring pens and soon was happily at work sketching flowers all over one side of the living room. When she was finished, she wanted to do something else. She thought for awhile, and then she decided . . . have you any *idea* what she did next?

YES! She [action] and *then* she [action].

Oh, she was having a MARVELOUS time, the time of her life! Just then the telephone rang. It was a friend calling to invite her over. Susan couldn't wait to tell her all the wonderful things she had done, so she yanked off the cap, flung it on the living room floor, and ran out.

And so it happened that when Mrs. Glasser came home—Susan and Steve's mother—she found the cap lying in the middle of the living room. "I wonder where that came from," she thought. "I've never seen that before. Probably left by one of their friends. Those kids, always forgetting things!" And then, "Strange kind of cap," she thought. "Wonder what I would look like in something like that?" She picked it up, brought it to a mirror and put it on. All of a sudden she felt a chill running through her, and the next thing she knew she was shouting, "AGA-BOOG-A-WAY X-NAY-SNAZE-NAY!"

And then she felt odd, tingly, like she wanted to *do* something, something mischievous, something bold, something she had never done before. And what do you suppose Mrs. Glasser decided to do?

What do you think a mother would do to be mischievous?

YES SHE DID!

Then Mrs. Glasser remembered a very expensive dress she had seen in the local boutique. "I'm going to buy it," she decided. "And maybe a few sweaters, and a new coat, and

Repeat audience suggestions, choosing one.

Motion for audience to join in.

If there is hesitation, ask the audience again in a different way.

Repeat the suggestions, replying "Yes, she did,"or "She thought about that," and, if gruesome ideas come up, "I wonder if she thought about that."

a suit." Tossing the cap on the couch, she ran outside and drove off in her car.

A few minutes later Mr. Glasser came home, and he couldn't believe his eyes. The door was wide open and the house was a mess. There were drawings of flowers all over the living room wall [repeat the things that Susan and Mrs. Glasser did that would be noticeable].

Mr. Glasser sank down on the couch, utterly bewildered. His eyes fell on the cap. "Funny looking kind of cap," he said, and without even thinking he put it on. The next second, he was up on his feet, shouting, "AGA-BOOG-A-WAY   X-NAY-SNAZE-NAY!"

Motion for audience to join in.

He felt odd, tingly, he felt like a little boy again, anxious to do something mischievous, something bold, something he'd never done before. "I've always wanted to jump up and down on the sofa. Shall I? Why not?" And in his suit and tie, still clutching his briefcase, Mr. Glasser began jumping on the sofa. "What fun, what fun. Oh, this is fun!" Then with a devilish gleam in his eye, he decided to [action]. . .

Look to audience for suggestions. Select several

Almost as soon as Mrs. Glasser had driven around the corner, she thought, "Where am I going? What am I doing?" She turned the car around and went home. When she walked into the house, she was astonished to see her husband . . .

Fill in last of audience suggestions you have embellished upon.

"Take off that cap!" she screamed.

Just then Susan walked in. "Take it off, dad! Take off that old cap!"

Steve came down just then. Hearing the cries and seeing his father's astonished face, he ran over and snatched the cap off Mr. Glasser's head. They all stared at each other, then at the cap.

"This is what started all the trouble," said Steve, shaking the cap in the air. "The cap!"

"It was the cap," said Susan.

"The cap!" repeated Mrs. Glasser.

"Steve," asked Mr. Glasser, "Did you bring this cap here? I want you to take it out of this house. Take it back wherever you got it, right away."

"Aw, dad. All right." Steve went outside, jumped on his bike and rode all the way back to the Golden Gate Bridge. He ran down to the old army pier and threw the cap into the water. At first it floated on top of the water, almost as if it were grinning at Steve. Then it slowly sank, disappearing, as tiny bubbles floated to the surface.

Now I don't know if any of you like to go fishing, or if you ever fish near the Golden Gate Bridge. But if you do, and if you should happen to catch an old faded denim cap with a visor strangely new looking, I suggest you THROW IT BACK. But if you should decide to put it on, just to see for yourself what will happen, expect to hear yourself shouting,

"AGA-BOOG-A-WAY X-NAY-SNAZE-NAY!"

Motion audience to repeat refrain.

And then send me a letter about what happens next, because I'd sure like to know!

NOTES

This is an original story that was inspired one afternoon when I went for a walk with Susan Terris and she told me a story that she was working on. The plot of her story gave me the idea for "Aga-boog-a-way X-nay-snaze-nay." So, here is an example of how one good story sparks another.

DIANE WOLKSTEIN

The Magic Wings

Introduction

The goose girl in this story is amazed by the sight of the sudden appearance of the flowers of spring. Her joy is exhilarating and contagious. She laughs. She giggles. She turns about. In response to the miracle of creation she wants to do something wonderful and miraculous. She decides to fly.

The others—the grocer's daughter, the judge's daughter, the princess, the queen—respond to the goose girl's incredible wish. And they, too, yearn to do the impossible. The difference between the goose girl and those who follow her is that the former is reacting directly to life while the latter are reacting to another human's "idea." Yet all feel the joy and happiness of stretching beyond their earthly capacities.

The following is how I have told the story in recent years. It is, of course, subject to the audience, the environment, and my inventiveness that day.

I ask for five "strong" volunteers from the audience. As the hands go up, I list the five roles. Boys volunteer as readily as girls. I usually choose an adult for the queen because it is fun to have a mix of children and adults playing together. I carefully select a very lightweight child for the goose girl.

When the five are standing before the audience, I announce a dress rehearsal. (I learned about dress rehearsals from Michael Parent.) I encourage the participants as well as the audience to describe the characteristics of a goose girl (easy-going, happy, carefree), of a grocer's daughter (responsible, strong, practical), of a judge's daughter (know-it-all, smart, clever), of a princess (vain, snobby, graceful) and of a queen (tall, fussy, bossy).

I then ask each participant to try flapping their arms in the way that their characters would. Some catch on immediately; others need a few tries. I remind them that they have volunteered because they are strong, and that once they start to flap their arms, they must continue to do so until the end of the story. (Surprisingly enough, nine out of ten goose girls do, while one or two of the others often falter and need encouragement.)

NARRATIVE	AUDIENCE RESPONSE OR TELLER'S ACTION
There was once a little goose girl in China. She was a poor, ragged thing with no mother or father. She lived with her aunt, and every morning she led the geese out of the yard and up into the hills, and every evening she brought the geese back down to the yard.	

One day in spring as she led the geese up the hill, she saw a tiny crocus pushing its way out of the earth. She bent over and watched.

Bend down to imaginary crocus.

It seemed to grow before her eyes. The earth was damp. It had rained during the night. Then from the corner of her eyes she saw another crocus, and another. And another! She turned, and everywhere she looked, she saw new flowers pushing their way out of the earth.

Dart around spotting flowers here and there.

"Hello!" they seemed to call to her. "Hello! Hello!"

The little girl started to run here and there, greeting each new bud and flower.

"Hello! Hello!" they called to her from all over the hillside.

"Hello!" Lilies, irises, clover, buttercups. But she could not run fast enough to greet each of them.

Just then one of her geese flapped its wings and lifted itself into the air. Ah, she thought, that is what I need to see all the flowers—*Wings.* If I had wings, I could fly over all the hillside and greet the spring!

Her thoughts returned to the earth, and she saw a little brook nearby. Quickly she ran to the brook, and cupping some water in her hands, she wet her shoulders. Then she stood very straight in a sunny place and slowly began to flap her arms in the air.

Mime cupping water from brook and wetting each shoulder of the "goose girl" on stage, and cue her arms to fly by lifting each from the back and flying with them (if she hasn't already commenced flying on her own).

It happened that the grocer's daughter was on her way home from visiting a friend and passed the goose girl on the hill. When she saw the goose girl waving her arms up and down, she stopped.

"What are you doing?" she asked.

After saying, "she stopped," go right up to the goose girl, look straight in her face and say, "What are you doing?"

"I'm growing wings," [from goose girl.]

As cued earlier, goose girl should answer, "I'm growing wings."

"Growing *wings?*"

"Yes, I'm growing wings so I can fly."

"You can't do that," the grocer's daughter said.

"Oh yes," the goose girl replied. "I've watered my shoulders, and soon my wings will sprout and I will fly over the world to greet the spring."

"I don't believe it," the grocer's daughter said. But when she got home, she thought, If a goose girl can fly, certainly a grocer's daughter can fly.

She went into the store and poured some milk into a bucket. She went outside and wet her shoulders with milk, stood in the sun, and slowly flapped her arms up and down in the air.

A judge's daughter was about to enter the grocer's shop when she saw the grocer's daughter waving her arms up and down in the air.

"What are you doing?" she asked.

"I'm growing wings," [from grocer's daughter cast.]
"Growing *wings?*""
"Yes. I'm growing wings so I can fly."

Mime wetting the shoulders of the grocer's daughter with milk, which ought to prompt her to fly.

As the judge's daughter, look straight up into the face of the grocer's daughter when you ask, "What are you doing?"

Note: Do not be surprised if she chooses to answer something other than, "I'm growing wings." Go with whatever is said, but return to story as soon as possible.

"You can't do that," said the judge's daughter.

"Oh yes. The goose girl covered her shoulders with water, but I've covered mine with milk so my wings will sprout and I will fly over the world."

"I don't believe it," the judge's daughter said, and she went into the store. But as she walked home, she thought, If a grocer's daughter can fly, if a goose girl can fly, certainly a judge's daughter can fly!

At home she went down into the cellar, and looking for the oldest wine—wine is said to produce great miracles!—she poured a small amount into a glass and went outside. Then she wet her shoulders with the wine, stood in the sun, and slowly flapped her arms up and down in the air.

Mime pouring wine on shoulders of judge's daughter. Prompt her arms to fly if they haven't already begun.

It was tiring, but she continued. And the grocer's daughter in town continued, and so did the goose girl on the hill.

It was a lovely day, and the princess decided to take a stroll through the upper parts of the town. When she passed the judge's daughter standing on her terrace waving her arms in the air, she stopped.

"What are you doing?" the princess inquired.

As princess, look straight into the face of

"I'm growing wings," [from judge's daughter.]

the judge's daughter when you ask, "What are you doing?" Cast member (judge's daughter) will reply, "I'm growing wings."

"Yes. I'm growing wings so I can fly," said the judge's daughter.

"You can't fly."

"Yes, Your Majesty. The goose girl has wet her shoulders with water, the grocer's daughter with milk. But I have wet my shoulders with wine so my wings will sprout and soon I shall fly over the world."

"It is not to be believed," the princess replied. But immediately she thought to herself, If a judge's daughter can fly, if a grocer's daughter can fly, if a mere goose girl can fly, then certainly a princess can fly!

The princess returned to the palace. She went into her bedroom and poured her most precious perfume—does not perfume bring the gods to earth?—onto her shoulders. Then she stood on her balcony overlooking the town, and gracefully waved her arms up and down in the air. Waiting . . .

Mime delicately pouring perfume on the shoulders of the princess. Prompt the princess to fly if she has not already begun.

The queen stepped out onto her balcony and saw the princess flapping her arms in the air.

"Purple cushions!" the queen exclaimed. "Whatever are you doing?"

"I'm growing wings," [from princess.]

Look straight into the face of princess when speaking to her.

When asked, "What are you doing?" cast member (princess) replies, "I'm growing wings."

"Wings? *To fly?* My dear, do you know what you are saying?"

"Yes! Yes! The goose girl wet her shoulders with water, the grocer's daughter with milk, the judge's daughter with wine. But I have wet my shoulders with the finest perfume, so *I* shall be the one to fly!"

"Purple—" and the queen was about to say "dragons!" when it occurred to her that she, the queen, had never flown, and what if the princess, or worse yet, the judge's daughter, should fly before the queen?

The queen turned on her heels and strode through the palace to the royal treasury, where the sacred oil for crowning kings, queens, and emperors was kept. With brief ceremony and dignity, she anointed her shoulders with oil Then she went out onto her balcony and began to flap her arms up and down in the air. Waiting . . .

Mime regally pouring oil on the shoulders of the queen. Queens always tend to begin flapping without prompting.

114

When the girls and women of the town saw and heard about what the princess and queen were doing, they stopped what they were doing and wet their shoulders. Soon all the girls and women were standing in a sunny place, flapping their arms in the air. Waiting . . . .

"Sister!"

"Mother!"

"Wife!"

"Grandma!"

The boys and men beseeched the girls and women.

"Speak to us!"

"Explain to us!"

"Tell us. What are you doing?"

But the girls and women were concentrating all their efforts on flapping their arms so they might fly.

In desperation the men and boys appealed to the Spirit in Heaven Who Grows Wings. The Spirit in Heaven Who Grows Wings heard their cry and had sympathy for their plight. It was impossible for life to continue happily, with the girls and women waiting eternally to fly.

The Spirit Who Grows Wings considered the matter and determined that one should be permitted to fly. But which one?

The Spirit descended to earth.

The Spirit flew from one girl to another, from one woman to another. The scent of the princess greatly attracted the Spirit, yet it could not be denied that certain grandmothers *were* trying very hard. The Spirit surveyed each girl and woman—the goose girl, the grocer's daughter, the judge's daughter, the princess (oh! the smell of the princess!), the queen . . . and at last the Spirit came up behind—

The little goose girl!

The goose girl felt a trembling behind her and a trembling all about her. A wind came. And suddenly she was sailing in the air, higher and higher and higher. She saw crocuses and lilies, roses and lady slippers, violets and daisies, star grass and buttercups—

The waiting was over. The goose girl who had wanted to greet the spring had been choosen. And all the people ran into the meadow to watch her fly.

"It's spring!" the birds sang.

Keep an eye on the cast as well as the audience. Give any tired flyers a boost by getting behind them and raising their arms in HIGHER movements.

If necessary, encourage the audience to participate by pulling a few from their seats.

Encourage *everyone* to join in.

Move around in search of one likely candidate to allow to fly. Stop behind the goose girl.

Lift goose girl in air from waist or under shoulders, whichever is easier, and carry her around the room for the ending.

115

"It's spring!" the people shouted.

"Hello!" the flowers called to the goose girl.

"Hello! Hello!" she called back. "It's spring!"

[Note: The original tale had only females flying, but there is no reason the sexes cannot be mixed—Judge's son, etc.]

NOTES

I begin with the song Shirly Keller wrote (see song below) and teach it to the participants and the audience. Once the audience has learned the song they feel more a part of the story.

I begin the story . . . "There was once a little goose girl," and motion for each participant to mime the gestures as her part is described in the story. Sometimes I help them by scooping up water from the earth to put on the goose girl's shoulders or patting milk on the grocer's daughter's shoulders. Usually by then, the other participants catch on and some voluntarily speak up.

I repeat the refrain, encouraging the audience to join in, by pausing before each phrase. "The goose girl put *water* on her shoulders, the grocer's daughter put *milk* on her shoulders, the judge's daughter put *wine* on her shoulders . . . ."

After the queen has put oil on her shoulders, I look directly at the audience and say, "When the girls and women of the town saw and heard about what the princess and queen were doing, they stopped what they were doing and wet their shoulders." Then I gesture for the audience to stand up and flap their arms. I leave the participants and walk among the audience, admiring their flapping and speaking to them, "What do you have on your shoulders?" "Do you think you might be the one to fly?" I continue the story from the audience.

At the words, "The scent of the princess," I return to the participants and make my way behind the participants, coming up behind the little goose girl! I lift her high in the air (whispering to her to keep flapping, the child is usually rather shocked) and improvise the ending. Hello little flowers, hello trees. It's spring! Welcome! Welcome! It's spring!

My way of telling is just one possibility. If you choose to tell this story of the little goose girl, I hope, in the telling, you will discover other possibilities.

Happy Telling! Happy Springs!

IF I HAD WINGS

© 1983
Words & Music by Shirley Keller

NOTES ON CONTRIBUTORS

Carol L. Birch

Carol L. Birch has been called "the best shortstory teller, and the best, short storyteller . . .with the timing to know the difference." Tell she does, while juggling jobs as a professional storyteller, director of recordings for Weston Woods Studios and for the National Association for the Preservation and Perpetuation of Storytelling (NAPPS), adjunct faculty member at Wesleyan University, and consultant on innumerable media productions. Her most recent audio tape of stories, *Happily Ever After: Love Stories...More or Less*, was recognized by the American Library Association as one of 1987's Notable Recordings.

Heather Forest

Heather Forest is a nationally acclaimed storyteller whose minstrel style of storytelling interweaves original music, movement, poetry, and the sung and spoken word. Her unique retellings of traditional tales from around the world have delighted audiences of all ages in schools, theatres and folk festivals throughout the United States.

Heather has recorded three albums of storytelling: *SONGSPINNER: Folktales and Fables Sung and Told*, which won an American Library Association Notable Record Award; *Tales of Women Folk*, a collection of folktales featuring courageous and resourceful heroines; and *Sing Me a Story: Musical Folktales for Children*. She has also published a book, *The Baker's Dozen ...A Colonial American Tale*, illustrated by Susan Gaber (Harcourt, Brace Jovanovich).

Linda Goss

Linda Goss was born and raised near the Smoky Mountains in Alcoa, Tennessee. She remembers with fascination the stories her parents and Grandfather told her. Award-winning, internationally-known storyteller Linda Goss has been featured on the Today Show, in *The New York Times, The Washington Post, The Philadelphia Inquirer* and *Essence* magazine. She was featured on the cover of *Learning* magazine and on that magazine's poster pull-out. She has performed across the country to sold-out audiences, most recently at the National Storytelling Festival at Jonesborough, Tennessee, the Smithsonian and the Kennedy Center. Named the Official Storyteller of Philadelphia, Goss is the co-founder of the In the Tradition National Festival of Black Storytelling and the president of the Association of Black Storytellers as well as co-founder of Hola Kumbaya, a cultural arts organization. In addition, Goss is storyteller-in-residence sponsored by the Pennsylvania Council on the Arts and currently teaches storytelling to adults at the Please-Touch Museum in Philadelphia. In the recent past, the mayors of Washington, D.C., and Alcoa, Tennessee (Goss's home-town) proclaimed Official Linda Goss Days. She is married to playwright Clay Goss.

Bill Harley

A professional storyteller for the past ten years, Bill has performed up and down the East Coast at schools, coffeehouses, camps and festivals. Relying primarily on original material, he creates a landscape of American life filled with baseball players, lumberjacks, monsters in the plumbing, first loves and coyotes.

Raised in his early years in Ohio, Bill moved to the East Coast during high school and later attended Hamilton College in Clinton, New York.

To date, he has released five recordings on his own label. Round River Records: *Monsters in the Bathroom* (1986); *50 Ways to Fool Your Mother* (1986); *Dinosaurs Never Say Please* (1987); *Cool in School* (1987); and *Coyote* (1987).

Gail Neary Herman

Gail Herman calls herself an "organic storyteller" because the stories she tells change and grow naturally with each audience interaction. She uses mime, movement, and music to entice audience members to help shape stories—through images, actions, and fantasies—so that they become truly "tales of the folk."

Dr. Herman has taught storytelling at many universities, including Wesleyan University and Eastern Connecticut State University. At present she teaches at the University of Connecticut, in the CONFRATUTE program, and at Frostbury State University in Maryland. She received her doctorate in Curriculum and Instruction at the University of Connecticut, and holds master's degrees in both Theatre and Aesthetics of Education. She has taught at the elementary level for seven years and coordinated a program for the gifted and talented for three years.

In addition, she directed the first two State Student Storytelling Festivals in Connecticut and West Virginia. Her book, *Storytelling: A Triad in the Arts*, was published by Creative Learning Press. A tape including "Juan Bobo and SiSi" is available from the author.

Ruthilde Kronberg

Ruthilde Kronberg has been a professional storyteller for twelve years. Through her, thousands of youngsters have confronted the age-old questions of ethics and heroism posed by classic fairytales and legends. By using puppets she helps children to lose their inhibitions, and soon they are well on their way to answering these questions for themselves and to finding new solutions.

Ruthilde began telling stories as a nurse in Germany. Her experiences in World War II have made her aware of the consequences of inhumanity. Asked why she tells stories, Ruthilde says, "It is a way to teach children to think and to make choices."

Her husband and her two eldest sons Peter and Andreas have created many of her puppets. Her son Michael often illustrates the stories while she tells them. Her daughter Miriam has used many of her stories while working with children who have special needs. Ruthilde hopes to leave a legacy of fine stories to her grandchildren.

Ruthilde works for Springboard to Learning, Young Audiences, and the Wilson School. She is the coauthor, along with Lynn Rubright and Luise Ulmer, of the book, *The Bible Tells Me So*.

Kaye Lindauer

Kay Lindauer obtained her undergraduate degree in Child Development, her master's degree in Child Development and School Library (MLS). She is an associate for Children's Literature, School of Information Studies at Syracuse University and teaches graduate courses in Children's Literature, Media for Children, and Storytelling.

Kaye has been an elementary school librarian (three years) and, for the past eight years, a middle-school librarian for the Fayetteville-Manlius School District, where she has been active in promoting storytelling clubs and festivals. In addition, she coordinates the annual "Clever Gretchen" conference on folklore literature and stories at Syracuse University.

Doug Lipman

Doug Lipman is a storyteller and a musician who has performed and given workshops from coast to coast. As a former nursery school teacher, he says, "I learned to use participation in self-defense. I had twenty pre-schoolers who would only listen if they had a way to join in." As a music teacher, he had already learned and developed techniques that allowed children of all ages to participate in music. Doug applied those same techniques to storytelling; his unique blend of "warm and lively songs" is the result.

Doug has recorded two tapes of participation stories with songs for young children: *Keep on Shaking,* and *Tell It With Me,* which won a Parent's Choice Award.

Norma Livo

Norma J. Livo was raised in western Pennsylvania with Pennsylvania Dutch and Scotch-Irish family influences. Stories, music, raccoons and imagination were always an integral part of her life growing up. She married a man from Finland, had four children, and learned to add Finnish stories and family stories to her storytelling collection. She earned a doctorate from the University of Pittsburgh.

She is currently a professor at the University of Colorado at Denver. She organized a special interest storytelling group with the International Reading Association. Norma is the coauthor, with Sandra A. Rietz, of three books on storytelling: *Storytelling Process and Practice* (1986), *Storytelling Activities* (1987), and *Storytelling Folklore Sourcebook* (in press), all published by Libraries Unlimited. She has organized and directed a Rocky Mountain Region Storytelling Conference for the past twelve years and teaches courses on storytelling at the University of Colorado at Denver. She has also been part of a troupe called Storytellers on Tour that tours rural towns of Colorado each fall telling stories in schools, libraries, and other community settings. She serves as regional representative for the National Association for the Preservation and Perpetuation of Storytelling (NAPPS) and also is on the editorial board for *The National Storytelling Journal.*

Her grandchildren are experienced storytellers and so the tradition continues.

Teresa Miller

Teresa Miller is certified as a Performing Artist in the Schools by Teacher's College, Columbia University. Through her workshop, "Why Every Teacher Should Be a Storyteller and How To Do It With Minimum Learning Pain," her desire is to spark teachers into using stories "to give children a decent chance at a rewarding life as an adult." She considers her experience as a writer, executive secretary, office manager, administrator, publicist, and travel agent the best life-preparation for storytelling. She is currently working on *Joining In II - An Anthology of Participation Stories for the Holidays.* It will include stories for major holidays such as Christmas and Hanukkah and minor holidays such as April Fool's Day. She is interested in hearing from folks with stories that they would like considered for inclusion.

Anne Pellowski

Anne Pellowski grew up on a farm in Wisconsin, in a community of Polish Americans whose ancestors arrived in the U.S. just before the Civil War. After attending the College of Saint Teresa and studying on a Fulbright at the International Youth Library in Munich, Germany, she entered Columbia University Library School and became a trainee at The New York Public Library. In 1957 she took the in-service training given by Augusta Baker and has been a storyteller ever since, having told in libraries, city parks, schools, hospitals, penal institutions, museums, theatres, universities and many other places. Most important has been the storytelling within her large, extended family. She has told stories in over 60 countries and 45 states, and tells in Spanish, French and German as well as English. She is the author of *The World of Storytelling* (Bowker, 1978), *The Story Vine* (Macmillan, 1984), *The Family Storytelling Handbook* (Macmillan, 1987) as well as numerous other books and recordings.

John Porcino

In September of 1981, half way into a 3,000 mile bicycle tour of the U.S., in a school along the Mississippi River, John Porcino told his first story as a storyteller. When the children "roared" back at him, he discovered for the first time the magic of telling stories.

During the next few years the art of storytelling became an increasingly important tool in John's work as a naturalist, kindergarten teacher, and camp counselor/director.

John is currently a full-time professional storyteller/folksinger and has shared his colorful repertoire of tales to enthusiastic audiences from pre-school to adults at schools, libraries, festivals, radio and television stations, museums, coffeehouses, churches and conferences throughout America. His performances include the Hudson River Sloop Clearwater's Pumpkin Sail, the Boston Children's Museum, Artpark's Storytellers Place, the Peoples Voice Cafe Greenwich Village NY, The New England Artist Festival, and the Three Apples Storytelling Festival. He is a recording artist for Story Stone Cassette Magazine. He also is part of the organizing boards of the Eastern New England Storytellers Guild, The Stories for World Change Network, The League for Advancement of New England Storytelling, and The New Song Library.

George Shannon

After many years of traveling about the country telling stories in the oral tradition, George Shannon has exchanged external journeys for internal ones at his writing desk. His nonfiction works include *Folk Literature and Children* (Greenwood), *Storytelling* with Ellin Greene (Garland) and various essays that examine the relationship betwen listener and teller, reader and writer. He has published nine books for young people, including *Dance Away* (Greenwillow), *Oh I Love* (Bradbury), and *Sea Gifts* (Godine). His novel for young adults entitled *Unlived Affections* (Harper & Row) explores the ways in which the stories we choose to tell either weave our lives into designs or tie them into painful knots.

Laura Simms

Laura Simms is a storyteller, poet and teacher who researches stories from all over the world, as well as composing her own. A professional performing artist for twenty-one years, she has appeared in theaters, festivals, schools and universities all over the U.S. and abroad.

In 1967 she graduated from SUNY in Binghampton, New York, with honors in literature and history, and one year later began her career in dance and theater. In her work as a storyteller, Laura combines her dance/theater background with her knowledge in literature, history, myth, anthropology and psychology.

A founding member of the New York City Storytelling, she also serves as a consultant, advisor, and board member for many institutions, including the National Association for the Preservation and Perpetuation of Storytelling (NAAPS).

Her recordings include: *Stories: Old as the World, Fresh As the Rain* (Weston

Woods, 1979); *Incredible Journey* (A Gentle Wind, 1979); *Just Right for Kids* (Kids Records, 1984); *There's a Horse in My Pocket* (Kids Records, 1987); and *Moon on Fire* (Yellow Moon Press, 1987).

Frances Stallings

Fran Stallings grew up in a tradition of family storytelling. Although she got her degrees in biology (that's another story), she has been a professional storyteller since 1978. To her repertory of over 200 myths, legends, and tales from all parts of the world she has added historical narratives and an increasing number of original stories, some with songs accompanied by Appalachian autoharp.

In her home state of Oklahoma she has touched thousands of K-12 students as an artist-in-residence with the State Arts Council. She reaches thousands more through workshops which train teachers and librarians in curriculum applications of storytelling.

Fran conducts residencies, workshops, and festival performances nationwide. She was an instructor at the National Association for the Preservation and Perpetuation of Storytelling (NAPPS) 1988 Summer Storytelling Institute, and serves on the resource review committee for NAPPS' catalog of tapes and books.

Fran lives in Bartlesville, Oklahoma, with her husband and two children. A founding member of Territory Tellers, Oklahoma's storytelling guild, she edits their quarterly "Territorial Tattler." When she is not travelling she writes professional articles and fiction. Her work has appeared in publications including *National Storytelling Journal, Instructor, Gifted Child Monthly, Aurora, Redbook*, and overseas translations.

Ruth Stotter

Ruth Stotter, a profesional storyteller with an interdisciplinary M.A. in Storytelling from Sonoma State University, California, has performed all over the U.S. and in England and Australia. Ruth teaches beginning and advanced storytelling classes and conducts numerous workshops, including "Enhance the Sending: Tips, Techniques, Games and Exercises," for all levels of storytellers. In 1987 she conducted a workshop, "Storytelling with Props: Puppets, Masks and More!" at the annual conference of the Puppeteers of America. She directs the Dominican College Storytelling Certificate program in San Rafael, California, and produces and hosts "The Oral Tradition," a weekly radio program in San Francisco. Ruth's published articles include: "The Kinesic Component of Storytelling," "Storytelling: Bridge Between Cultures," and "Spinning Tales from Corn-Silk." She presented a paper at the 1985 American Folklore Society, "Interpretive Performance of Traditional Native American Oral Narratives," and in 1986 was invited to participate in a panel on telling Jack Tales. She also produced The Storyteller's Calendar for 1988 and 1989, which "delights teachers, storytellers, librarians and all who toil in the vineyards of oral tradition."—*COME-ALL-YE* .

Diane Wolkstein

After graduating from Smith College, Diane Wolkstein chose to become a professional storyteller, unheard of at that time. Twenty-three years ago, she told Bible stories in Paris. Since then, she has told at elementary schools, colleges, festivals and museums throughout the United States, Canada, and abroad. In America, she was among the pioneers who began the "Revival Movement" (of storytelling), and encouraged the National Association for the Preservation and Perpetuation of Storytelling (NAPPS) to enrich their program by offering workshops for storytellers.

She is the author of twelve books on folklore and mythology. Two of her books, *The Magic Orange Tree and Other Haitian Folktales* (Schocken) and *White Wave: A Taoist Tale from China* (Crowell) were American Library Association notables. Diane is also a recording artist, and has made twelve audio cassettes and two video cassettes. Her audio and video cassettes are available from: Cloudstone, 40 South Middletown Road, Montvale, NJ 07645.

Contacting Contributors

All of the contributors to this book are storytellers who are involved in teaching classes, leading workshops, and giving performances throughout the U.S. If you would like information on any of these activities from a teller, contact them at their address below. They will be happy to send you information on the programs and workshops they offer. Many of the contributors have produced tapes and/or records, as well as authored books (this information is provided in the individual entries above).

Carol Birch
20 Blueberry Hill Road
Weston, CT 06883

Heather Forest
P.O. Box 354
Huntington, NY 11743

Linda Goss
c/o Hola Kumba Ya
P.O. Box 50173
Philadelphia, PA 19132

Bill Harley
301 Jacob Street
Seekonk, MA 02771

Gail Herman
Route 2, Lodge Circle, Sky Valley
Swanton, MD 21561

Ruthilde Kronberg
608 Bacon
Webster Groves, MO 63119

Kaye Lindauer
4907 Briarwood Lane
Manlius, NY 13104

Doug Lipman
P.O. Box 441195
West Somerville, MA 02144

Norma Livo
11960 West 22nd Place
Lakewood, CO 80215

Teresa Miller
226-03 141st Avenue
Laurelton, NY 11413

Anne Pellowski
210 Riverside 9J
New York, NY 10025

John Porcino
253 Long Plain Road
Amherst, MA 01002

Barbara Reed
Old Quarry
Guilford, CT 06437

Laura Simms
814 Broadway
New York, NY 10003

George Shannon
725 1/2 Hudson Street
Eau Claire, WI 54703

Frances Stallings
1406 Macklyn Lane
Bartlesville, OK 74006

Ruth Stotter
P.O. Box 726
Stinson Beach, CA 94970

Diane Wolkstein
10 Patchin Place
New York, NY 10011

Further Resources

There are numerous regional storytelling organizations and excellent workshops which take place all over the country which it would be impossible for us to list here. So, we are listing the National Association for the Preservation and Perpetuation of Storytelling (NAPPS), the major national organization, as the best way to keep informed of what is happening and as a resource to find out about organizations in your area. NAPPS issues a national directory of storytelling annually, which lists storytellers, conferences, organizations, and newsletters. They have a resource catalog of books and tapes, which are for sale, and issue a quarterly magazine for its members *The National Storytelling Journal* , which contains interesting articles and information about storytelling. Their address is: NAPPS, P.O. Box 112, Jonesborough, TN 37659.

Yellow Moon's catalog contains over 175+ books and tapes by a wide range of tellers and authors. We will be glad to send you one on request.

We are committed to publishing material directly related to the oral tradition/spoken word. It is our goal to make available material that both explores the history of the oral tradition and breathes new life into it. In order to provide a comprehensive selection of materials our catalog includes, in addition to Yellow Moon Press titles, a large number of titles that are published by individual tellers and other publishers.